Other titles published in association with the National Association for Special Education Needs (nasen):

Language for Learning in the Secondary School: A Practical Guide for Supporting Students with Speech, Language and Communication Needs
Sue Hayden and Emma Jordan
2012/pb: 978-0-415-61975-2

ADHD: All Your Questions Answered: A Complete Handbook for SENCOs and Teachers
Fintan O'Regan
2012/pb: 978-0-415-59770-8

Assessing Children with Specific Learning Difficulties: A Teacher's Practical Guide
Gavin Reid, Gad Elbeheri and John Everatt
2012/pb: 978-0-415-67027-2

Using Playful Practice to Communicate with Special Children
Margaret Corke
2012/pb: 978-0-415-68767-6

The Equality Act for Educational Professionals: A simple guide to disability and inclusion in schools
Geraldine Hills
2012/pb: 978-0-415-68768-3

Dyslexia and Inclusion: Classroom Approaches for Assessment, Teaching and Learning
Gavin Reid
2012/pb: 978-0-415-60758-2

Brilliant Ideas for Using ICT in the Inclusive Classroom
Sally McKeown and Angela McGlashon
2011/pb: 978-0-415-67254-2

More Troub

There are many factors that can contribute to the learning difficulties children and adults have with mathematics. These include poor working memory, difficulties in retrieving the so-called 'basic' facts and the ability to remember and apply formulas and procedures correctly.

This highly practical teacher resource is for anyone who would like to accurately and effectively identify mathematics learning difficulties and dyscalculia among their pupils. Written in an engaging and user-friendly style, Steve Chinn draws on his extensive experience and expertise to:

- show how to consider all the factors relating to mathematical learning difficulties;
- explain how these factors can be investigated;
- explore their impact on learning;
- discuss and provide a range of tests ranging from pre-requisite skills such as working memory to normative tests for mathematics knowledge and skills.

The book will guide the reader in the interpretation of tests, emphasising the need for a clinical approach when assessing individuals, and shows how diagnosis and assessment can become part of everyday teaching. This resource also includes pragmatic tests that can be implemented in the classroom, and shows how identifying the barriers to learning is the first step in setting up any programme of intervention.

Steve Chinn has previously been founder and Principal for 19 years of an award-winning specialist school for dyslexics. He was also Head of two other specialist schools and a mainstream teacher for 14 years. He is now an independent international lecturer, writer and researcher. He has also published with Routledge *The Trouble with Maths, second edition* (2012).

nasen is a professional membership association that supports all those who work with or care for children and young people with special and additional educational needs. Members include teachers, teaching assistants, support workers, other educationalists, students and parents.

nasen supports its members through policy documents, journals, its magazine *Special!*, publications, professional development courses, regional networks and newsletters. Its website contains more current information, such as responses to government consultations. **nasen's** published documents are held in very high regard both in the UK and internationally.

More Trouble with Maths

A complete guide to identifying and diagnosing mathematical difficulties

Steve Chinn

Routledge
Taylor & Francis Group

LONDON AND NEW YORK

Helping Everyone Achieve

First published 2012
by Routledge
2 Park Square, Milton Park, Abingdon, Oxon OX14 4RN

Simultaneously published in the USA and Canada
by Routledge
711 Third Avenue, New York, NY 10017

Routledge is an imprint of the Taylor & Francis Group, an informa business

British Library Cataloguing in Publication Data
A catalogue record for this book is available from the British Library

Library of Congress Cataloging in Publication Data
Chinn, Stephen J.
More trouble with maths : a teacher's complete guide to identifying and diagnosing mathematical
difficulties / Steve Chinn.
p. cm.
 1. Mathematics—Study and teaching. 2. Mathematical ability—Testing. I. Title.
QA11.2.C475 2012
510.71—dc23

2011048983

ISBN: 978-0-415-67013-5 (pbk)
ISBN: 978-0-203-11739-2 (ebk)

Typeset in Helvetica
by Cenveo Publisher Services

MIX
Paper from
responsible sources
FSC® C004839
www.fsc.org

Printed and bound in Great Britain by the MPG Books Group

Contents

Foreword

This is an astonishing book! 'Troubles with maths' are both varied and widespread; difficulties with maths in school cause anxiety and not only affect educational achievement but also limit career prospects. It follows that the early identification of problems with number, followed by appropriate intervention, should be a priority for all industrialised societies. But knowledge of how to assess mathematical difficulties is poor despite a growing evidence base on the nature and causes of 'dyscalculia'. In this book, Steve Chinn shares many years of expertise with extreme clarity; assessment needs to be the first step to intervention and the book provides a comprehensive explanation for the practitioner of what is needed in order to properly understand mathematical learning difficulties. At the core of the book is a test protocol that goes well beyond a screening instrument. The assessment incorporates background information, teacher observations and a questionnaire probing maths anxiety as well as more conventional tasks tapping basic number knowledge, number facts, numerical operations and reasoning skills. It also includes standardised assessment procedures that have been developed by the author, together with sample diagnostic reports, generously shared. This book should be on the shelves of all professionals in the field of maths education and educational assessment and I am confident that it will spearhead a much needed increase in proficiency in the assessment of numeracy skills in the field.

Maggie Snowling
University of York
November 2011

1 Introduction – dyscalculia, mathematics learning difficulties and the test protocol: How the protocol is designed around our understanding of maths learning difficulties and dyscalculia

This book was written to complement *The Trouble with Maths: A practical guide to helping learners with numeracy difficulties* (Chinn, 2012). It looks at assessing and diagnosing learning difficulties in mathematics and links those processes to the teaching philosophies and pragmatics in *The Trouble with Maths*.

It contains:

- a diagnostic protocol;
- a norm-referenced (UK sample∗) 15 minute mathematics test for ages 7 to 59;
- norm-referenced (UK sample∗) tests for the four sets of basic facts (+ − x ÷) for ages 7 to 15;
- a norm-referenced (English sample∗) anxiety, 'How I feel about mathematics' test of mathematics anxiety for ages 11 to 16 (a version for adults is available on my website, www.stevechinn.co.uk);
- a test of thinking cognitive (thinking) style in mathematics;
- a dyscalculia checklist;
- informal tests for vocabulary, symbols, place value, estimation;
- a structured, exemplar test of word problems;
- informal tests of short-term memory and working memory;
- guidance on how to appraise the ability to estimate;
- guidance on how to use errors and error patterns in diagnosis and intervention;
- guidance on how to construct criterion-referenced tests and how to integrate them into day-to-day teaching;
- case studies.

∗Samples for each test were over 2000.

The tests and procedures in this book should enable teachers and tutors to diagnose and identify the key factors that contribute to learning difficulties in mathematics and dyscalculia. There are many examples in which the relationships between topics reinforce the need to take a broad and flexible approach to diagnosis and assessment.

Dyscalculia

This book is about assessing and diagnosing mathematics learning difficulties and dyscalculia. It takes the view that mathematics learning difficulties are on a spectrum. At the severe end of the spectrum, the learning difficulties might be labelled as 'dyscalculia'.

This book is also about the evidence that might be collected, evaluated and analysed to make decisions about mathematics learning difficulties, their causes and their severity.

The definition of dyscalculia, a specific learning difficulty, published by the UK's Department of Education and Skills (2001) states:

> Dyscalculia is a condition that affects the ability to acquire mathematical skills. Dyscalculic learners may have difficulty understanding simple number concepts, lack an intuitive grasp of numbers and have problems learning number facts and procedures. Even if they produce a correct answer, or use a correct method, they may do so mechanically and without confidence (p. 1).

Kavale and Forness (2000) wrote a critical analysis of definitions of learning disabilities. Their observations and the problems of building a diagnostic procedure around a definition, as I think is proper, lead me to think that a fully satisfactory definition of dyscalculia has yet to evolve. In the meantime, the definition above will suffice as a working version.

Thambirajah (2011) has suggested four criteria for diagnosis of dyscalculia. They are:

1   Difficulties with understanding quantities or carrying out basic arithmetic operations that are not consistent with the person's chronological age, educational opportunities or intellectual abilities.
2   The severity of the difficulties is substantial as assessed by standardised measures of these skills (at the 5th percentile of achievement) or by academic performance (two school years behind peers) and is persistent.
3   There is significant interference with academic achievements and the activities of daily living that require mathematical skills.
4   The arithmetic difficulties are present from an early age and are not due to visual, hearing or neurological causes or lack of schooling.

There are a couple of observations to make on these criteria. First, the use of the word 'chronological' does not infer that mathematics achievement levels continue to increase throughout our age span, but it is more relevant to the age of students when at school. Second, the choice of the 5th percentile is somewhat arbitrary, but does match the general/average level quoted in research papers on dyscalculia, for example, Ramaa and Gowramma's (2002) study found that 5.54% of their sample of 1408 children were considered to exhibit dyscalculia.

Professor Brian Butterworth's 'Dyscalculia Screener' is computer based and could be used to supplement the evidence collected via the tests and procedures in this book (and vice versa!)

What is mathematics? What is numeracy?

It is valuable to know what we are assessing, whether it is arithmetic, mathematics or numeracy. These are terms that we often use casually. Although such 'casually' is adequate in most cases, it may be useful to look at some definitions of these words. The task is not as easy as one might hope. Authors of 'mathematics' books often avoid the challenge. For a subject that often deals in precision, the definitions are not a good example.

In England we frequently use the term 'numeracy'. We introduced a 'National Numeracy Strategy' for all schools in the late 1990s, defining numeracy as:

> a proficiency which involves confidence and competence with numbers and measures. It requires an understanding of the number system, a repertoire of computational skills and an inclination and ability to solve number problems in a variety of contexts. Numeracy also demands practical understanding of the ways in which information is gathered by counting and measuring and is presented in graphs, diagrams, charts and tables.
>
> *(DfEE Framework for Teaching Mathematics: Year 7, 1999)*

However, as if to illustrate how we use these words interchangeably, the DfEE explained that the National *Numeracy* Strategy would be implemented by schools providing a structured daily *mathematics* lesson.

Wikipedia defines numeracy as:

> the ability to reason with numbers and other mathematical concepts. A numerically literate person can manage and respond to the mathematical demands of life— Aspects of numeracy include number sense, operation sense, computation, measurement, geometry, probability and statistics.

A different perspective was given, somewhat controversially, by Michael Girling (2001) who defined basic numeracy as: 'the ability to use a four function electronic calculator sensibly (p. 12).'

I have taken two definitions of mathematics from online dictionaries to add to our understanding:

> Mathematics is the study of numbers, shapes and space using reason and usually a special system of symbols and rules for organizing them.
>
> *(Cambridge dictionary online)*

and

> the study or use of numbers and shapes to calculate, represent, or describe things. Mathematics includes arithmetic, geometry, and algebra.
>
> *(Macmillan dictionary online)*

The assessment and diagnostic tools in this book primarily address arithmetic, that part of mathematics that focuses on numbers and the four operations: addition, subtraction, multiplication and division. I am working on the assumption (and experience) that this is where the majority of mathematics learning difficulties are rooted, certainly at the dyscalculia level.

Mathematics learning difficulties

If dyscalculia is at the severe end of a spectrum of mathematics learning difficulties, then there are going to be difficulties above that threshold, hence the use of the term mathematics learning difficulties (MLD). These difficulties, such as dyscalculia, continue to be a problem beyond school age, which suggests that they are perseverant and/or resistant to current teaching methods.

The term MLD is often used interchangeably with 'developmental dyscalculia' in the USA (for example, Mabbott and Bisanz, 2008). In the USA MLD are estimated to affect 5–8% of school-aged children (Geary, 2004). There is, of course, a difference between the use of the word 'disability' and the use of the word 'difficulty'. I am working with the term, mathematics learning difficulties and am taking that to refer to the bottom 20–25% of students in terms of achievement in mathematics. Some support for this assertion is to be found in studies on adults, for example:

In a large-scale survey of a sample of adults aged 16–65 in industrialised countries, the International Adult Literacy Survey, the UK came third from bottom for 'quantitative literacy' (OECD, 1997, quoted in Coben, 2003). Quantitative literacy is defined as, 'the knowledge and skills required to apply arithmetic operations to numbers embedded in printed materials' and is a term used in the USA for numeracy. More than one-half the UK adult population is estimated to be performing below the minimum level required to cope with the demands of life and work, with 23.2% at the lowest level (Level 1) and 27.8% at Level 2.

Rashid and Brooks (2010) in their study, *The Levels of Attainment in Literacy and Numeracy of 13- to 19-year Olds in England, 1948–2009*, noted that 22% of 16- to 19-year olds are functionally innumerate and that this has remained at the same level for at least 20 years.

A further piece of evidence of the perseveration of the problem with lower achievers in mathematics comes from Hodgen et al., (2010) and their 30-year comparison of attainment in mathematics in secondary school children:

> A further rather worrying feature is that in all three topic areas (algebra, decimals and ratio) and all year groups there are now a higher proportion of very low performances than there were in 1976/7. It is difficult to explain this; one possibility is the closing of many Special Schools and greater inclusivity within the mainstream sector. However it is not clear whether this factor could account for the full size of the difference. Another possible explanation lies in the finding that the National Numeracy had the effect of depressing attainment at the lower end, perhaps because of the failure to address children's particular needs in attempting to provide equal access to the curriculum (p. 8).

The findings were somewhat sensationalised by the *Sunday Times* (11 September 2011) with a headline: 'Number of clueless maths pupils soars.'

Many of the problems surrounding mathematics are international, for example, Ramaa and Gowramma (2002) found that 25% of the children in their sample of 1408 primary-aged Indian pupils were considered by their teachers to have arithmetic difficulty.

Learning difficulties in mathematics can be caused by many factors, with each factor contributing a variable influence that depends on many things, such as the mathematics topic or the current level of anxiety in the individual. Some of the factors are attributed to the person, for example, a poor working memory, some are external, for example, inappropriate instruction (more detail is provided in Chapter 2, 'The Trouble with Maths').

Thus, learning difficulties in mathematics are a complex problem and any diagnosis will reflect the situation on the day and time when it is carried out, although a thorough procedure should usually produce much useful and valid information. One consequence of this complexity and the many contributory factors is that the approach to assessment/diagnosis should always be multi-dimensional and flexible. A second consequence is that there will be the inevitable spectrum of difficulties. This should not be a revelation to any educator. We should expect a wide variation in children and adults and for the normal distribution to apply.

A further implication of the heterogeneous nature of mathematics learning difficulties is that there will be no prescribed order of structure for the assessment or the subsequent intervention. For example, it may be that for one person there are anxiety issues that have to be addressed before any action can be taken on their cognitive issues. For another person, it may be that the investigation has to be targeted initially at a particular mathematics topic so that a particular barrier can be overcome and success experienced. Ultimately all the factors will interlink.

Tests and testing

This book contains a number of tests. They are included, of course, to contribute to the assessment and diagnosis. However, tests have to elicit answers to be of any use. The classic reaction of the anxious, low confidence learner is not to attempt the task (Chinn, 1995). The assessment has to be carried out in a way that creates at least a basic level of confidence and relaxation in the subject.

Should you have concerns about test anxiety, there is a test anxiety inventory for children and adolescents, the TAICA (Whitaker Sena et al., 2007).

Tests are a snapshot of 'now' and are influenced both by many factors that we may suspect are present, such as anxiety, and by factors that we may not fully appreciate are present, such as the influences of past experiences of learning mathematics. We need to remember that testing is something that you do *to* the student, whereas diagnosis is something you do *with* the student. So, the book contains a range of materials that will help the process of diagnosis.

If you are about to undertake an assessment/diagnosis, then there are some questions that might guide what and how you carry out that task.

Some basic questions

For each component of the assessment/diagnosis, the leading questions are:

- What do you want to know?
- Why do you want to know it?
- How will you investigate it?

Then more targeted questions should include:

- How severe is the problem?

  You may want to know the mathematics age or the percentile at which the subject is performing. This will require an appropriate norm-referenced test. Knowing the severity of the deficit may attract resources to help address the problem.

- What can't he do?

  It is important to know where the gaps are so that the intervention can be directed efficiently. For example, there may be issues with procedures, working memory, language or speed of working. Problems may have their origin a long way back in the roots of arithmetic.

- What can he do?

  Intervention will be most effective if it starts where the learner is secure. The protocol must focus on the strengths as well as the weaknesses. For example, addition seems to be the default procedure for many people who are weak at mathematics. Finding topics that 'he can do' can be used to give a rare experience of success for the learner.

- What doesn't he know?

  There are two facets to this question. One is the USA's National Research Council report (2000) on how people learn which had three key findings. Part of the second finding is that students need 'a deep foundation of factual knowledge'. For some 'traditionalists' this means that students should be able to retrieve from memory (quickly) all of the times table facts. If 'not knowing' these facts is made into an issue, then not knowing them may become part of the problem of learning mathematics. There is also substantial evidence, for example (Nunes et al. (2009) and Ofsted (2006)) that the dominant way of teaching mathematics in the UK is by memorising formulas.

  The other facet is to define what exactly constitutes a 'deep' foundation of knowledge. In other words, what do you *need* to know (and what can you work out)?

- What does he know?

  Intervention should start where the learner's knowledge and, it is hoped, understanding is secure. Sometimes it may be necessary to question what seems to be known rather than understood. A good memory can take you a long way in basic mathematics! (But understanding is better.)

- How does he learn?

  The process of learning is far more complicated than the process of memorising. I suspect this statement applies to teaching as well. There are many factors associated with this four-word question. These may include the cognitive style of the learner (Chapter 10), his working memory (Chapter 5), his response to materials, that is does he need to start at the concrete stage of learning?

- How can I teach him?

  It would be sensible to teach him the way that he learns. Much of this concept is covered in *The Trouble with Maths* (Chinn, 2012). One of the objectives of a diagnosis is to find out the way the student learns.

- What does the learner bring?

  A learner can bring emotional baggage, a lot of anxiety, poor self-efficacy and a long history of failure at mathematics. In an on-going informal survey of teachers around the UK and in many other countries, teachers are stating that enough children are giving up on mathematics at age 7 to be noticed in a class. So, an adult aged 19 may have many years of failure behind them.

- Where do I start the intervention?
    This is another key question. The answer is usually further back than you might initially think. The answer to this question has to be another key objective for the diagnosis to answer.

A diagnostic protocol

Chinn (1991), working with the Dyslexia Institute's Mathematics Skills Committee, suggested a structure for diagnosis that included:

1 a standardised (norm-referenced) mathematics age;
2 an assessment of the child's ability to recognise and use mathematics symbols;
3 an assessment of basic fact knowledge, compensatory strategies and understanding of numbers and their relationships;
4 cognitive style;
5 the level of understanding of place value;
6 mathematics language;
7 a measure of his or her accuracy in calculations;
8 an assessment of understanding and accuracy in using algorithms (procedures and formulas);
9 a measure of speed of working;
10 an analysis of error patterns;
11 a test of ability to solve basic word problems.

Later this was modified (Chinn and Ashcroft, 1993) to include attitude and anxiety, money and mathematics language.

The structure of this protocol forms the basis for the work in this book. Of course, it has been further refined and modified over the following 20 years, with, for example, the importance of the role of working memory now being recognised.

It seems to be important that the tests and procedures included in this book are practical and pragmatic. They have been chosen because they can generate information that will help in the assessment and provide diagnostic clues as to how intervention can best be provided for each individual. The tests and activities, with the exception of the tests for working and short-term memories are directly about mathematics. There is no need to extrapolate any findings.

Three norm-referenced tests have been produced by the author specifically for inclusion in this book. Also included is a test of thinking (cognitive) style, which was written by the author and colleagues John Bath and Dwight Knox and published in the USA (Bath et al., 1986).

One of the goals of this book is to make the interpretation of tests more realistic, maybe even intellectually cynical. The process of assessment/diagnosis is there to help a child or an adult, not to provide data for performance comparisons and political points.

It is about finding out why there are difficulties and what can be done to address those difficulties.

Mathematics learning difficulties and individuals

The realisation that children with learning difficulties in mathematics are a heterogeneous group is not new. For example, in 1947, Tilton noted that 'some children fail owing not to carelessness or simple ignorance, but because of individual misconceptions of rules, and a lack of grasp of number concepts'. Austin (1982) observed, 'perhaps the learning disability population simply includes too diverse a student population to make teaching recommendations unique to this group'. Chinn and Ashcroft (2007) consider that the interactions between the factors that can contribute to learning difficulties in mathematics create an enormous individuality among dyslexic learners.

There are a number of individual reasons and even more combinations of reasons why a child or adult may fail in mathematics. The implication from this should be that there will need to be both a range of interventions available to teach to those individual profiles and an equally diverse set of diagnostic tools which are used in a responsive and adaptable diagnostic protocol.

Teaching and diagnosing

The two activities, teaching and diagnosing, should be inextricably linked. Each should inform the other, hence this volume and its complement, *The Trouble with Maths*. One book is on diagnosis and the other is on teaching. The relationship between diagnosis and teaching is an example of the chicken and egg dilemma. The answer may not be quite appropriate to a biologically sound solution for the chicken or the egg, but for intervention and diagnosis, the two should be concurrent.

Further reading

Chinn, S. (2011) *The Fear of Maths and How to Overcome It*, London: Souvenir Press. (A book written for older learners, adults and parents.)

Chinn, S. (2011) 'Mathematics learning difficulties and dyscalculia', in *Special Needs. A Guide for Inclusive Practice*, Peer, L. and Reid, G. (eds), London: SAGE. (The chapter gives a more comprehensive view of the topic.)

2 Diagnosis, assessment and teaching: The benefits of interlinking

'Be better than the test you use.'

(Alan Kaufman)

Diagnosis, assessment and teaching should always be interlinked and should be on-going. Assessment can be used to identify problems with learning and diagnosis should lead to ideas for understanding and addressing those problems, but, more importantly both can be used to pre-empt many future problems with learning mathematics. As far as is possible we need to get teaching right first time to capture the powerful influence of the first learning experience.

Assessment is an integral part of teaching and learning.

(Primary School Curriculum, Ireland, 1999)

And so is diagnosis.

Assessment is about measuring the student's achievements, skills and deficits. It's about knowing what the student can do and her level of performance and knowledge, usually in comparison to a peer group.

Diagnosis is about going beyond what a learner can and cannot do, identifying how he learns, what and why he is not learning or why he is underachieving. It should also lead to advice on appropriate intervention.

It is our view that diagnosis is a data collection procedure for determining instructional needs.

(Underhill et al., 1980: 12)

We have to remember two influences that may help us decide which data to collect and how to collect it:

Whereas **cognitive ability** reflects what an individual can do, **personality traits** reflect what an individual will do.

(Hattie, 2009: 45)

Brueckner and Bond (1955) explain three levels of diagnosis:

1 General diagnosis is the use of comprehensive survey tests and other general evaluation procedures. This could be seen as 'assessment'.
2 Analytical diagnosis is the use of systematic procedures for locating and identifying specific weaknesses.
3 Case study diagnosis is the application of clinical procedures that provide for a detailed study of the performance or achievement of an individual pupil with an

evident learning problem so as to determine as specifically as possible the nature and seriousness of the learning difficulty and the underlying causes.

The tests and diagnostic activities included in this book can be selected and combined to access all three levels, although the goal is to provide materials for a thorough diagnosis and that will include some assessment tools.

Assessment

Assessment may be carried out to compare the learner's achievements with his/her peers or to identify the mathematics he can do and understand and the mathematics he cannot do and understand. The first objective can be achieved via a norm-referenced test (NRT) and the second may need the additional information provided by criterion-referenced tests (CRTs).

My first degree was in chemistry where I learnt about the Heisenberg Principle. I am taking what it stated, on a sub-atomic scale and applying it to testing. The Principle says that what you measure you change, because the process of measuring has an influence on the quantities you are trying to measure. On a human scale, there is a risk that the act of measuring changes the level of response, usually negatively, and this is often due to the process of measuring creating debilitating anxiety.

For example, one of the bigger challenges in compiling material for this book was the task of collecting data for the 15 minute summative test from adults. Many adults do not want to spend up to 15 minutes doing a mathematics test as a favour to someone they don't know. I achieved a little more success with adults by renaming the 'Mathematics Test' a 'Mathematics Survey'.

Norm-referenced tests

> A standardised test is administered and scored according to specific and uniform procedures. When standardised tests are used to compare performance to students across the country they are called 'standardised norm-referenced tests'.
>
> *(Kubiszyn and Borich, 2007: 349)*

Thus, a NRT is a test that has been given to a suitably large, representative sample of children and/or adults. The scores from the sample are examined and analysed. A teacher using the test can then compare his students' results with the norm-referenced results. This should give a measure as to how far ahead or behind a student's performance is compared to his peers. NRTs are often used to measure progress (but see later) or the current state of students' learning and achievement.

Kubiszyn and Borich (2007) advise that 'the information obtained from a NRT is usually not as useful for classroom decision making as the information obtained from CRT's'. If the opportunity is there, using both types of test will lead to the most useful information.

Sometimes people use the term '*summative* evaluation' to describe the measurement of achievement. Summative evaluations are usually normative.

The questionnaire below may help when selecting a NRT. There are no definitive answers to the questions. Using the questionnaire is about helping you to identify the test that most closely matches your specific needs.

Questionnaire for selecting a norm-referenced test

Starting with four general questions:

1   What do you need from the test?
2   Is it for screening a group?
3   Is it part (hopefully not all) of a diagnosis?
4   Is it to measure progress?

And the 13 more specific questions:

- Is it a test which is restricted in use to psychologists (that is, not available for teacher use)? (For example the WISC, the Weschler Intelligence Scale for Children, may only be used by psychologists. There are some sensible reasons for this to be the case.)
- How much does it cost (a) initially and (b) for extra test sheets and score sheets?
- What does it look like? (For example, are the items too close together? Is the font clear? Does its appearance overwhelm the subject? Is it age-appropriate in appearance?)
- How much time does the test take? (There will be a compromise between a test being thorough enough to give a valid measurement and being too daunting, taking up too much of the often limited endurance span of the subject and leaving enough time to investigate other facets and components of learning while the subject is not too tired mentally to perform at a level that is typical of his/her ability.)
- What age range is the test designed for? (In terms of curriculum content, a norm-referenced test is by its nature a sampling test. It should include enough items from across the curriculum to give a picture of overall achievement. Setting up a test could be viewed as a statistical exercise in that the items that are included in the test are there because they contribute to the normal distribution of scores for the test, not just because they are testing a particular procedure [which would make them criterion-referenced items as well]. By restricting the age range, the range of topics can be reduced which can make the test shorter or make it more thorough in examining the topics it does cover.) There is a potential problem in using restricted age ranges. If the student is, say, 15-years-old, but working at the level of 10-year-old, the test that matches the achievement level may look as though it has been designed to interest a 10-year-old, which is not motivating for a 15-year-old. The test may display its target age on the front cover. This is not likely to motivate a 15-year-old student. A small age range may make short-term comparisons more reliable, but may impede long-term monitoring.
- Can it be read to pupils? (Remember that you're testing mathematics not reading. However, reading the test to the student may invalidate the use of test data that has been collected under standardised conditions. If the student cannot read the test, the words not the symbols, then my inclination is to read it for them. A non-reader is not going to be able to display the mathematics he knows if he

cannot access the words. Note that the norm-referenced test in Chapter 8 has few words.)

- How many items for a one-year gain of mathematics age? (One year's progress could be just two items on some tests.)
- How often do you wish to assess progress? Does the test have a parallel form? (These questions follow on from the previous question.)
- Does it match you mathematics curriculum? (Are you testing what your students have been taught?)
- Do the individual items test what they are intended to test? (For example, 33×251 may test long multiplication, whereas 79×683 may only expose inadequate recall of times tables facts.)
- Can you extract any diagnostic information? (The answer to this question is usually 'Yes', even if the test precedes or instigates your diagnostic procedure.)
- What are the details of the sample used to collect the norm-referenced data? (The reason for producing a norm-referenced test is so that a subject's performance can be compared to that of his peers. The data for this comparison will have been collected from a sample of children and/or adults. The pertinent questions are: (a) How many in the sample? (b) Where from? England? The UK? Abroad? (c) When was the data collected? [How long ago?])
- Is there a balanced mix of thinking/cognitive styles in the questions? (This may not be a valid question for all tests.)

There are a number of tests for teachers to use that are available in the UK and other countries. It may not be a wide choice and when the questions above have been answered, that choice may become even more restricted.

Remember that testing is not an exact science, particularly when interpreting the test results from one individual. Students' attitudes and performances may be labile. You could have set the test on a bad day for a pupil. Also the average score for a group may mask many individual variations. For example, an average score may not always be achieved from the same combination of questions.

Having chosen your test, using it will confirm, or disprove your choice. Sometimes using a test with your students will be the only way to make the final decision. Of course, a curriculum change may make your choice redundant, but this may not necessarily be the case, for example, despite the changes introduced by the National Numeracy Strategy in the UK, the actual mathematics content is much as it ever was. This is usually the situation (with the possible exception of the somewhat bizarre foray into 'new' mathematics some years ago, which destroyed what remained of parental confidence in trying to help their children with mathematics homework).

It is not unusual for people with learning difficulties to be relatively slow processors. This means that they may not have enough time to demonstrate all their knowledge within the time limits set for a standardised test. One strategy to deal with this problem is to give the subject a different coloured pen (or change pen for pencil) when the time limit is up so that they can continue until they have done all that they can. The different coloured writing identifies what was done after the time limit.

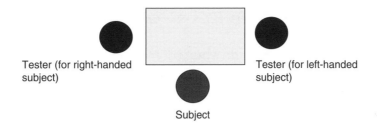

Figure 2.1 Seating places for observation

Whichever NRT you chose, if you are using it with an individual, then it helps if you, the assessor, can sit where you can observe the subject at work, actually see them as they write. This also means that you need to be familiar with the tests you use so that you can focus on observing the subject as he works in order to pick up all the non-verbal clues, such as finger counting, sub-vocalising, order of working through a problem, where pauses occur and anxiety (see Figure 2.1). This advice applies to all the tests and activities described in this book.

My experience of carrying out an individual, 'one-off' assessment/diagnosis leads me to believe that the time for which a subject can sustain effective concentration on mathematics tasks in these intensely focused one-to-one circumstances is around 1 hour. One implication from this is the length of time that can be devoted to using a standardised test within the assessment/diagnosis. For example, the 'Profile of Mathematical Skills' (France, 1979) takes around 3 hours to complete (it was not designed to be attempted in one session) and is obviously not suitable for these circumstances. The shortest test that is commercially available in the UK as I write this book is the WRAT 4, which has a time allowance of 15 minutes. It has norm-referenced data for a huge age range (from 5 years up to 94 years 11 months). The data is from the USA. The NRT in Chapter 8 of this book also has a 15-minute time limit, but has UK norms.

There is, obviously, in terms of using NRTs, a compromise. A longer test should provide a lot more information and should lead to a more secure assessment of the mathematics achievement age. A longer test can provide a more comprehensive coverage of mathematics topics and may have a second item for some topics, so that the evaluations of answers are not drawn from one example alone. However, a shorter test used in the circumstances of a diagnostic protocol may have one specific purpose, that is, to obtain a measure of 'mathematics age/achievement level', to know how the subject compares to his or her peers. Other information can be obtained from other tasks.

So, in a full, one session only, assessment/diagnosis it is likely that the test chosen will have to be what is known, somewhat cynically, in the USA as a 'quick and dirty' test.

However, even a short test may give some diagnostic information. The 15-minute mathematics test provided in Chapter 8 includes several items that have been selected and trialled before the data for norm-referencing was collected so that they may lead to some diagnostic information. The selection of items was about maximising the information that could be gathered within the endurance limits of the subject being assessed.

Why do you test? Some reasons for testing

When teachers ask me 'What test do you recommend?' I ask 'What do you want to find?' and maybe 'Why are you testing?' (I realise the answer to the second question may well be 'Because X told me to.')

There are a number of reasons why we might test. These include:

- A teacher may wish to monitor the progress of his or her group and/or identify those who need extra help and/or collect data with which to stream groups.
- Parents may wish to know how their child's achievements compare with those of his peers.
- There may be a need to measure rates of progress of individuals and groups.
- To evaluate the efficacy of a mathematics programme/scheme.
- There may be some mandatory requirement to test for entry to a profession.
- The test may be used to assess the ability of the pupil to progress to higher levels of study or to a new school.
- To provide information for an educational statement of special needs (which may lead to extra provision and resources for the student).
- To provide evidence for concessions/special provisions for examinations.
- The test may be used to award a certificate recording a level of achievement (for example, the GCSE, the General Certificate of Secondary Education, a UK qualification, usually taken at age 16).
- It may be used for diagnostic reasons (for example, to find the student's strengths, weaknesses, knowledge base and learning style) and thus inform teachers on how to provide effective intervention.

When and how often to use a norm-referenced test in classroom situations

In order to compare gains made over 12 months, you may have to test twice a year. The summer break is a great opportunity for mathematics skills and knowledge to slip away and thus for test scores to decay. Mathematics is a set of skills and, like any set of skills, performance will deteriorate in the absence of practice. Therefore, any testing done at the start of the academic year is likely to show lower performance scores from those achieved in tests done at the end of the previous academic year.

Testing at the end of the academic year should show the maximum score for that year for any individual, but it will be too late to be of diagnostic value in terms of guiding intervention.

A good compromise may be to test at the start of the academic year, when the test could provide useful diagnostic information, both for individuals and for the class group, by highlighting weaker areas that can then be addressed before new work is introduced. The areas that have declined over the summer break may well be areas where learning is fragile and thus in need of top-up revision. By analysing the results, for the group and for the individuals who are causing concern, intervention can be delivered more effectively and efficiently. For example, if, say 60 per cent of the group show a weakness in a particular topic then a group intervention is efficient. If only 5 per cent of the group show a problem in a particular task, then more individualised intervention is appropriate.

And then test half way through the year, which will show mid-year progress (though remember just how discriminating your test really is) and show if the deficits identified at the start of the year have been rectified. It should also identify any student who is regressing. Testing in mid-year also allows for comparisons of test scores over two equivalent 12-month periods.

In summary, then:

1 Test at the start of the academic year.
   Analyse the results to show areas of weakness in the class group and in individuals. Plan interventions.
2 Test mid-year to indicate the progress of individuals and the group.
   Analyse the results for the group and for individuals to show areas of strength and weakness and to screen for students who are not making progress.
3 Compare results for 12-month intervals to show progress from mid-year to mid-year and start of year to start of year for the group and for individuals.
   Identify the students who are not making progress. Appraise the effectiveness of teaching methods.

Using a commercially produced test does not remove the need for a teacher to be observant and analytical. I was privileged to hear Alan Kaufman, a world expert on testing, speak at a conference in Sweden in 2002. I asked if I could use the following quote from his talk, which I think summarises what we should always have in mind:

"Be better than the test you use".

Criterion-referenced tests

We believe that the preferred practice in diagnostic testing is for teachers to develop criterion-referenced tests that exactly parallel the curriculum being taught.
(Salvia and Ysseldyke, 1988: 525)

A *formative evaluation* is diagnostic in nature. Formative evaluations are usually criterion referenced. CRTs are dealt with in detail in Chapter 13.

Skills for diagnosis

1 Empathy.
2 To be able to select the appropriate tests and activities from the list outlined in Chapter 1 for the test protocol and to be able to do that responsively as the diagnosis proceeds. This infers that you have all the test materials to hand, that you have a test, equipment and activity 'library' or 'tool kit'.
3 The ability to observe empathetically, meticulously and objectively. This infers that you have complete familiarity with all the tests and activities that you might use and that you are able to spend the maximum time observing, writing pertinent notes on pre-prepared observation sheets.

4   The ability to ask diagnostic questions that are low stress for the individual being assessed. A useful question is 'Can you show me how did that?' expressed in a way that encourages a response from the individual.

5   An understanding, not just a knowledge or recall, of the mathematics you are testing, the ways it may be taught and learnt and the reasons why students may fail.

It is possible to extract diagnostic information from almost any mathematics work, but the extent and accuracy of your diagnosis will increase dramatically if you are able to see the learner working and can ask questions as he works. Sometimes errors are obvious (for example 32.6 − 4 = 32.2). Sometimes they are impossible to identify unless you can ask the key diagnostic questions, 'Can you tell me how you did that?' or 'Can you talk me through the method you used?'

Ongoing diagnosis

Diagnosis does not necessarily mean sitting down with a student for an hour or more, going through a lot of mathematics tests and activities. It can be an on-going process with information coming from written work and occasional pertinent questions, possibly prompted by observations of marked work, slowly building the picture, but also influencing and changing that picture with interventions following on from the diagnostic observations. The Chapters 9, on error patterns, and 13, on CRTs, will give some guidance for these issues.

I am a great believer in this on-going diagnosis, building diagnostic opportunities into lessons. Worksheets and homework can be designed and structured to include some diagnostic questions, perhaps questions that expose particular errors or misconceptions or show flexible and creative problem solving skills. Hopefully, this may make the goal of on-going diagnosis not too onerous even when working with a large class of children. Such carefully constructed worksheets, homework and class tests can offer information on individuals and, from the results for the whole group, useful feedback on your efforts at teaching that topic or, if you need to rationalise that concept away, then it could be a judgment of the curriculum! It should lead to a more informative record of progress than just a collection of marks out of 10.

Building up such resources will not be a short-term objective. It could be a cooperative venture for all the teachers who teach mathematics in the school or college and a good opportunity to identify and discuss common areas of concern.

Feeding back the results of the diagnosis

Feedback may be to a parent or carer, or a teacher, or a school, a funding authority or the student or all of these. This implies that you have to write the report about the diagnosis very carefully and accurately, so that it communicates effectively with all those parties. Having solid evidence is thus very important. Speculations are not desirable. Writing a report, and indeed the diagnostic process itself, is a great responsibility.

It is likely that the pupil or adult who is the subject of the diagnosis has had a long history of negative feedback. It would be good if both the verbal and written feedback were given in a way that did not add to that history.

3 The Dyscalculia Checklist: 31 characteristics that can lead to maths failure

This chapter looks at some of the more frequent manifestations and indicators of dyscalculia and discusses the significance of the 31 indicators that make up the Dyscalculia Checklist.

There are a number of key behaviours and concepts that are highly significant for anyone who is trying to learn mathematics. Some of the 31 indicators listed in this chapter are at the very fundamental level of arithmetic and some relate to more advanced levels, but any could create potential barriers, intellectual and emotional, to learning mathematics.

The implications of these indicators are explained, why they are included, what they contribute to the diagnosis and what they suggest for intervention.

The 31 items can be used as a screening survey of mathematics learning difficulties and dyscalculia. If the responses are discussed with the learner then the list can lead to information on how the learner thinks about mathematics, how the learner perceives mathematics and how intervention may be matched to the learner.

The list can be given to the learner for completion, or to a parent or a teacher, or to all three for comparison. Obviously, without the potential for discussion, there will be less information and evidence.

There is not a definitive score that defines a person as dyscalculic. Obviously if 30 or 31 characteristics are identified as issues, that would be a strong indication of a problem! The protocol offers other sources of further evidence.

1. Find it impossible to 'see' that four objects are 4 without counting (or 3 objects, if a young child)

The skill of being able to know how many dots there are in a randomly arranged cluster is called 'subitising' or 'dot enumeration' and is considered to be a key pre-requisite skill for numeracy by Butterworth (1999). In Butterworth's (2003) Screener, a randomly organised number of dots are presented on a computer screen and the subject's response is gauged for accuracy and response time. The number of dots that a person can see and just know 'how many' is around 4 or 5. Beyond this number it is likely that the dots will be held in visual working memory and counted. This strategy may take the number of dots up to 6 or 7. Learners with dyscalculia will perform below these levels.

This is also a test of number sense, knowing the quantity. Children could be taken from a concept of 'more' or 'less' to quantifying as a technique for developing this skill. Cards with dots could be compared. 'Which card has more dots?' 'Which card has less dots?'

2. Have difficulty counting objects accurately and lacks the ability to make 'one to one correspondence'

A failure to master this skill can create an early insecurity and inconsistency with numbers and thus handicap the development of number sense. Patterns for learning will be built more securely if what is being learned is consistent.

Mathematics begins with counting. It introduces the association of a number name with a quantity. It is a first experience of adding, adding one more object at a time. If the learner cannot coordinate and link the movement to the name, then learning the number sequence and its meaning will be unsuccessful.

Children may learn number sequences, perhaps by rhyme and this may give the illusion that the child 'knows' numbers.

3. Find it much harder to count backwards compared to counting forwards

This is partly to do with consistency. Learners seek consistency and counting backwards is different to counting forward. The quantity is getting smaller each time. Practice may be a factor in that we are much more likely to practise counting forwards than we are to practise counting backwards.

This behaviour can also indicate an inherent problem with changing to a reverse process. We often assume that if a process can be done forwards then the ability to 'do it backwards' occurs automatically. This is not necessarily so. Such assumptions may overlook the problems that some learners experience.

The difficulty could be rooted in problems with working memory. In the early stages of working on this skill, before it becomes automatic, the learner may have to use working memory by holding the forward sequence in memory and visualising (or 'hearing') the previous number.

In the same way that counting on sets the foundation for addition, this skill sets the foundation for subtraction. Counting backwards is about subtracting one at a time.

4. Count on for addition facts, for example, for 6 + 3, counts on '7, 8, 9' to get the answer

If a learner persists with counting in ones then number sense will not develop, neither will addition skills, and thus multiplication and algebra and many other mathematics skills. Therefore, this is a significant indicator of mathematics difficulties. Many of us will continue to use counting in some circumstances, for example, working out which day it will be in four days time, but we are not dependent solely on counting. Mostly, we learn to work in 'chunks'.

Counting in ones may indicate a developing inchworm style of learning (see Chapter 10). A secondary consequence of the impact on developing a sense of number is that this dependence will seriously handicap the development of estimation skills. Inchworm thinkers tend not to be comfortable with estimation.

Counting is a tempting strategy. It works. It is reasonably quick for the basic addition and subtraction facts and it keeps the learner in his comfort zone. Learning new topics often involves risk; the risk of failure. Weaning a learner off counting will take time. It should not be a cold turkey approach of 'You will not count.'

If there are concerns from items 1, 2 and 4 in this list, then the inference has to be that the learner will find mathematics difficult unless these concerns are addressed. This will be discussed after items 5 and 6.

Visual (and tactile) experiences may help wean the learner off an over-reliance on counting. Clusters of objects, set out in a consistent and developmental pattern will address some of the problems associated with poor subitising skills. The materials that may help include bead strings, counters, coins, base 10 (Dienes) blocks. For example, work on patterns may help the recognition of quantities and the interrelationship of quantities. The patterns have to interrelate if this is to be efficacious. The six pattern on dice and playing cards does not relate visually to the five pattern nor to the seven pattern.

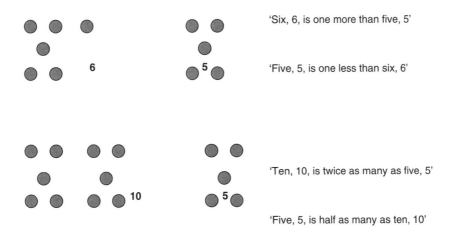

'Six, 6, is one more than five, 5'

'Five, 5, is one less than six, 6'

'Ten, 10, is twice as many as five, 5'

'Five, 5, is half as many as ten, 10'

A bead string can put numbers into a 10 perspective and a five perspective if two colours are used.

Six as one more than 5, as 5 + 1, as 4 less than 10, as 10 − 4. (Turning the string around illustrates the commutative property of addition, 6 + 4 = 4 + 6.)

5. Have difficulty with retrieving addition facts from memory

There are many basic facts, 121, on a 0 to 10 addition fact square. A child with a reasonable memory may remember many of them or count them very quickly and thus give the illusion of learning and knowing. Using strategies that link facts and the operations develops understanding, particularly when the key numbers (0, 1, 2, 5, 10) being used are 'comfortable'.

An example of relevant research, quoted in Boaler, (2009), by Gray and Tall (1994) highlights the use of strategies to compensate for an inability to retrieve facts from memory and how this relates to achievement in mathematics. In a study of 72 students aged 7–13 and the ways they accessed addition facts, they found a contrast between the above average and below average (at mathematics) students.

For the above average students:

- 9 per cent counted on
- 30 per cent known facts
- 61 per cent derived facts (use of strategies, other than counting)

For the below average students:

- 72 per cent counted on
- 22 per cent counted all
- 6 per cent known facts
- 0 per cent derived facts

Thus 94 per cent of the below average students were dependent on counting to access basic facts such as 6 + 7. They did not derive facts.

One of the components of the diagnosis process in this book is the 1-minute and 2-minute basic fact tests (Chapter 6). These are backed up by the informal items that investigate basic knowledge and skills (Chapter 4). In both activities there is an opportunity to ask the learner, 'How did you do that?' and thus investigate the use of strategies to derive facts, especially those that cannot be retrieved from memory. The use of strategies indicates a move away from a total reliance on counting.

6. Count all the numbers when adding, for example, for 5 + 3, counts '1, 2, 3, 4, 5 ... 6, 7, 8'

This behaviour shows a severe dependence on one-to-one counting. The learner cannot use, or see, the first number as a quantity, a starting quantity. Counting has to go back to the beginning, which suggests a poor concept of numbers.

Counting on the bigger number, as in adding 9 to 4 when given 4 + 9 shows an inability or reluctance to overview before starting to solve the problem. Again, numbers are not understood, merely subjected to immature strategies.

The implications of the continuance of counting in ones are significant for the development of mathematics skills. Addition is about adding numbers bigger than one, numbers in chunks. Multiplication is about adding a number of the same numbers, that is chunks of the same number, for example, 7 × 6 is about adding together seven lots of six.

The basic subtraction facts may cause even more difficulty, particularly if the dominant strategy is to count and the skill of counting backwards is not strong.

7. Find it difficult to count fluently sequences that are less familiar, such as: 1, 3, 5, 7 ... or 4, 14, 24, 34 ...

The skill of recognising and generating sequences and patterns demonstrates emerging number sense and the ability to see 'new' patterns, to move away from 'familiar' patterns. Patterns can help support poor long-term memories.

Sequences such as 4, 14, 24, 34, 44 … also reveal abilities with place value. Bead strings and coins are good materials for demonstrating these patterns.

8. Use tally marks for addition or subtraction problems

This suggests, again, a problem with moving on from counting in ones. The learner is not dealing with number as quantities (or chunks).

As the numbers the learner meets become bigger, counting in ones becomes increasingly inefficient. Mathematics is a subject that develops, with most concepts building on previous concepts. This development is partly about the efficiency in handling numbers. If the learner still uses tallies, a dependence on counting, then that efficiency, and probably accuracy, will not develop. Tallies indicate the lack of an ability to see and use the patterns of numbers. Often the tallies are just written one after another, with no grouping as with the 'gate' ⅢⅠ.

9. Have difficulty in progressing from the materials and images, for example, counters, blocks, tallies, to the symbols/numbers

This is likely to be a problem with cognitive development. The learner is stuck in the concrete operational stage of Piaget's developmental stages. It could also be an over-reliance on materials, in that the learner has not used the materials to enhance cognitive development. The materials represent consistency and security and may inhibit the progress to the formal operational stage.

Materials and images need to be linked to the symbols. This is not an automatic link for many learners. It should be made explicit. Follow-up investigations, which examine these links from the learner's perspective, may be helpful in the design of the programme of intervention.

Among the problems with this important transition to symbolic representation of mathematical information are the issues that involve mathematics vocabulary and place value. For example, base 10 blocks provide a clear illustration of 15, by showing a 10 block and 5 unit cubes in the order of the 10 block followed by the 5 cubes. The vocabulary is in the reverse order to the digits, '15'. The learner may not have developed automaticity with this inconsistency. A similar problem occurs with the similarity of the number sounds for '15' and '50', '16' and '60', and so on.

Materials can also interact with the language of 'early' operations. For example, 5 − 3 can be read as 'Five take away three', which could be demonstrated with five objects and then physically taking away three of them. Stern blocks could be used for 'What is the difference between five and three?' by placing a three block on top of a five block and noting the 'difference' which now has a mathematical meaning.

10. Have poor skills with money, for example, unable to calculate change from a purchase

This is a life skill, though increasingly machines are replacing any need to develop these skills. Calculating with money could also be seen as a cognitive variation on 'school' methods. Often estimation will suffice.

There is a need for the ability to select and use the mathematics relevant to the task. This item is about the learner having a sense of what the change from a purchase should be, so that could involve more than one calculation, for example, adding up the items on a restaurant bill, estimating the tip and then working out the change. Can the learner take any knowledge out of the classroom?

The problem may be exacerbated by the fact that notes and coinage are not proportional (in size) to the values they represent.

11. Think an item priced at £4.99 is '£4 and a bit' rather than almost £5

This is another example of interpreting numbers literally rather than demonstrating number sense and linking numbers to key values. As with Item 10, this is also a 'real life' skill, helping with estimation and comparisons.

Estimation skills depend on understanding base 10 and the decimal extension of base 10.

12. 'See' numbers literally and not as interrelated, for example, counts up from 1 to get 9, rather than using 10 – 1

This is extra evidence that suggests that there is an over-reliance on counting rather than understanding numbers, their values, how they interlink and the operations that manipulate them (Items 1, 2 and 6). It may also indicate a lack of appreciation of the role of 10 as a key number and as a key to understanding place value. Also it may relate to a difficulty with counting backwards (Item 3).

13. Find it difficult to write numbers that have zeros within them, such as, '304' or '4021'

Zero, 0, is a key concept in place value. It ensures all the 'places' are there even if there are, for example, no tens, as in 304, three hundred and four, or no units, as in 580, five hundred and eighty. Place value is a key concept in understanding the base 10, which underpins all understanding when learning mathematics. Learners need to know the implications of base ten and zero.

14. Find estimating impossible

There are two key issues here. First, if mathematics is taught as 'right' or 'wrong', a matter of being precise, then it should not be surprising that children do not adapt to the processes of estimation.

Second, some learners are only comfortable when things are literal, especially those with insecure number sense, so 9 is 9, not also 1 less than 10.

For some learners the process of estimation may be partially mastered, but they may have difficulty in knowing how to adjust the estimate to make it accurate without returning to a standard procedure. For example they may learn to relate 97 to 100 and add 536 to 97 as 536 + 100, but not be able to realise that an accurate answer involves subtracting 3 from the estimate (or then be able to carry out this adjustment). (See also Chapters 10 and 11).

15. Find it difficult to judge whether an answer is right, or nearly right

The ability to make such judgments is related to number sense and estimation skills. This situation is compounded by the problem that checking by a different method is not a natural skill, or indeed, inclination for many learners.

Often, the learner's emphasis is on process, not on outcome, so this could be another consequence of mathematics thinking style and also sense of number. It is rooted back to very early experiences of numbers. Unless these experiences have encouraged estimation and flexibility, then the (false) security of believing that a formula will automatically lead to an accurate answer every time will discourage the learner from judging the answer.

16. Organise written work poorly, for example, does not line up columns of numbers properly

This could be a consequence of co-occurring dyspraxia. It can have indirect implications in that untidy work may be judged less kindly, attracting lower marks. It can also have direct implications making operations such as lining up columns of numbers, setting out traditional 'long' multiplication, both of which are highly dependent on this skill. In a survey of 391 special education professionals in the USA, Bryant et al. (2000) list 33 behaviours of students who have teacher-identified mathematics weaknesses. Number 12 is 'Orders and spaces numbers inaccurately in multiplication and division' and number 13 is 'Misaligns vertical numbers in columns'.

One possible intervention is to provide squared paper, with square size tailored (via a photocopier) to match the writing of the individual. Vertical lines on the paper may also help.

17. Not 'see' automatically that 7 + 5 is the same as 5 + 7 (or that 7 × 3 is the same as 3 × 7)

Many of these characteristics are routed in sense of number and number operations (+ − × ÷). Apart from the fact that these two rules almost half the number of addition and multiplication facts that need to be learned, an understanding of the commutative rule is one of the foundations for understanding algebra.

18. Write 51 for 15 or 61 for 16 (and the same 'reversal' for all the teen numbers)

This is a classic example of the inconsistencies of early work on numbers. It is a quirk of the English language for numbers. The vocabulary is in the reverse order to the order in which the digits that make up the number are written.

It can also expose a problem with dual tasking (and automaticity) as this 'error' is likely to occur during a computation, when the learner is focusing on procedure as well as retrieving facts.

This problem is an illustration of the research of Buswell and Judd (1925) who noted that first learning experiences are influential in that what we learn when we meet a new topic is a dominant entry to our brain.

Another example of 'first learning' is set in the possibility that when children first meet subtraction they are told to 'Take the little number from the big number'.

19. Forget the question asked in mental arithmetic

Short-term memory is a key skill for all learning. Children with learning difficulties often have very poor short-term memories. They may only be able to hold 2 or 3 items/facts in their memory. Long and complicated (and 'complicated' is a relative term) questions may not be remembered or may be remembered inaccurately. The outcome for the learner is the same, an experience of failure.

It may well help if questions are modified in length and made more succinct and/or they are repeated completely and then just the first and/or key information is given. Learners may benefit from learning how to chunk information.

20. Struggle with mental arithmetic

This could be down to poor short-term memory. It could also be a consequence of poor working memory. And one of the key skills needed to be good at mental arithmetic is working memory. There is enough research (for example, Gathercole and Alloway, 2008: 39) to support this assertion.

An additional problem is the cultural expectation that answers will be achieved quickly. This is another problem for the learner who processes slowly. Having to answer quickly may increase anxiety and it has been shown that anxiety depresses working memory (Ashcraft et al., 1998).

21. Learn multiplication facts, but then forget them overnight

There is a wide-spread expectation that all children (and thus adults) can rote learn the times table facts. This is not so. This is even less so for dyslexic learners (Chinn, 1994) and almost certainly for dyscalculic learners. Many children struggle to learn facts after school and then those facts have disappeared from memory the next morning, which is both frustrating and de-motivating.

The facts that are most likely to be learned are the 2 ×, 5 × and 10 × (and the 0 × and 1 ×, though these can be more tricky than might be expected).

The culture of mathematics has traditionally believed that success in this task is possible for all learners. For example, an obituary for 88-year-old teacher in the teachers' weekly newspaper the *TES* (4 June 2010) noted that:

> He was the epitome of the village school master; he believed in times tables and the power of education. He was particularly keen on mental arithmetic, and demanded that his charges recite their times tables every day.

And from a 1998 English Government book:

> Further Activities: Things to do at Home
> TABLES: Choose a multiplication table that is problematic … .
> and learn it!   Learn to say it backwards too.

On a compensatory note for those who cannot achieve success in this task, being able to rote learn these facts does not automatically make you good at arithmetic. In fact it may create the illusion of learning, knowledge without understanding.

On a further compensatory note, it is possible to teach strategies for accessing these facts, using the key facts and the application of some basic mathematics principles. This may also help the learner to understand some later mathematics procedures and concepts (see *The Trouble with Maths* [Chinn, 2012])

If the learner has to go down the rote learning path then one of the most effective strategies for rote learning is self-voice echo (Lane and Chinn, 1986), but even this technique does not work for everyone. Basically the technique involves the learner recording facts in his/her own voice onto a PC and the looking at one fact as the voice is played back, repeatedly through headphones (www.self-voice.com).

22. Only know the 2 ×, 5 × and 10 × multiplication facts

As mentioned in Item 21 this is so often the case. It is, probably, the patterns and verbal clues that make these particular facts more memorable, but, as stated above, it is possible to learn how to use them to build all the other facts … and learn about key mathematics procedures, too.

23. Count on to access the 2 × and 5 × facts

This means that counting is still present as a base skill. The learner is not able to directly 'enter' the facts at, say, 7 ×. Although counting will lead to the fact, it is inefficient and if the fact is being used in a strategy to access another fact, then the counting may overload short-term memory. It is a disadvantage in mathematics if the key facts cannot be accessed. Other facts can be worked out, but you do need the key facts of $1 \times$, $2 \times$, $5 \times$ and $10 \times$ as automatically as possible.

24. Make 'big' errors for multiplication facts, such as $6 \times 7 = 67$ or $6 \times 7 = 13$

This is often the case with the low achievers. It demonstrates a lack of number sense and a lack of understanding of what multiplication 'does' to numbers. Higher achievers tend to give a close, but incorrect table fact, or a near to correct value answer.

There is no doubt that the ability to access the multiplication facts is very helpful in school-level mathematics. If the research on learning is consulted (Bransford et al., 2000) then the conclusions are:

Key Finding 2 (out of 3)
To develop confidence in an area of inquiry, students must:
    have a deep foundation of factual knowledge
    understand facts and ideas in the context of a conceptual framework
    and organise knowledge in ways that facilitate retrieval and application.

The 'deep foundation' of factual knowledge could have a minimum content of the key facts combined with an ability to use them to access the other facts.

Further evidence comes from a major study from New Zealand, a meta-analysis of hundreds of research papers (Hattie, 2009): 'The programmes with greatest effect were strategy based methods.'

25. Like to use formulas, but uses them mechanically without any understanding of how they work

This is a tempting and seductive situation for teacher and learners alike. Formulas are secure: but only if you remember them. It is also a key characteristic of the inchworm thinking style (Chapter 10).

26. Forget mathematical procedures, especially as they become more complex, such as decomposing, renaming, regrouping or borrowing for subtraction and, almost certainly, the 'traditional' method for division

Learning, if that is what it is, without understanding will result in forgetting what is learned whether it is facts or procedures. Research by Engelhardt (1977) noted that it is procedural errors that distinguish the low achievers from the high achievers. High achievers are unlikely to make procedural errors.

27. Get very anxious about doing any mathematics

'Mathematics anxiety' is recognised as a problem internationally. In my own research into anxiety (Chinn, 2009) in 11–17-year-old students, 'taking a mathematics exam' came top of the list with 'doing long division without a calculator' and 'having to do mathematics quickly' was also high up the list.

Chapter 7 is devoted to mathematics anxiety. The anxiety questionnaire in that chapter can act as a starting point for discussions about mathematics difficulties as well as identifying some of the main causes of anxiety.

28. Refuse to try any mathematics, especially unfamiliar topics

Mathematics is usually a matter of right or wrong, success or failure. Some learners wish to minimise the risk of failure and do so by not trying to do any questions or problems. In a study of errors made by dyslexic students, I (1995) found that the frequency of the 'no attempt' error was significantly higher for dyslexic students.

My more recent informal surveys of teachers, in the UK and internationally, suggest that enough children are giving up on mathematics at ages 6 and 7 for teachers to notice.

29. Become impulsive when doing mathematics, rather than being analytical – rushes to get it over with

This could be a sign of inability and/or a type of avoidance. It could also be an extreme application of 'procedural/inchworm' behaviour. The learner just invokes a formula without any thought of analysing the problem.

30. Show an inability to 'see' patterns or generalisations, especially ones that are incompatible with previous patterns, for example that 1/2, 1/3, 1/4, 1/5 is a sequence that is getting smaller

Patterns and generalisations support memory and understanding, but patterns that challenge previous consistencies need extra explanation. If learners do not absorb and understand new patterns it can be an example of resistance to new material and an over-security with (hard-won) existing knowledge. It can also suggest a weak ability to generalise and see patterns.

31. Think that algebra is impossible to understand

If the principles of number and the operations are not understood, then algebra will not be understood. The links are strong. For example, if the learner cannot progress from or recognise the link between

$6 + \square = 13$ to $6 + y = 13$, or $5 \times \square = 30$ and $5y = 30$ then algebra will not evolve from arithmetic.

Checklist for Dyscalculia

Name _____ Age _____ Date _____

Does the learner ... or Do you ...

☑ 1. Find it impossible to 'see' that four objects are 4 without counting (or 3 objects, if a young child)

☐ 2. Have difficulty counting objects accurately and lack the ability to make 'one to one correspondence'

☑ 3. Find it much harder to count backwards compared to counting forwards

☑ 4. Count on for addition facts, for example, for 6 + 3, counting on '7, 8, 9' to get the answer

☑ 5. Have difficulty with retrieving addition facts from memory

☑ 6. Count all the numbers when adding, for example, for 5 + 3, counting '1, 2, 3, 4, 5 ... 6, 7, 8'

☑ 7. Find it difficult to count fluently sequences that are less familiar, such as: 1, 3, 5, 7 ... or 4, 14, 24, 34 ...

☐ 8. Use tally marks for addition or subtraction problems

☑ 9. Have difficulty in progressing from the materials and images, for example, counters, blocks, tallies, to the symbols/numbers

☑ 10. Have poor skills with money, for example, unable to calculate change from a purchase

☐ 11. Think an item priced at £4.99 is '£4 and a bit' rather than almost £5

☑ 12. 'See' numbers literally and not interrelated, for example, count up from 1 to get 9, rather than using 10 – 1

☐ 13. Find it difficult to write numbers that have zeros within them, such as, '304' or '4021'

☑ 14. Find estimating impossible

☑ 15. Find it difficult to judge whether an answer is right, or nearly right

16. Organise written work poorly, for example, not lining up columns of numbers properly ☑

17. Not 'see' automatically that $7 + 5$ is the same as $5 + 7$ (or that 7×3 is the same as 3×7) ☑

18. Write 51 for 15 or 61 for 16 (and the same 'reversal' for all the teen numbers) ☐

19. Forget the question asked in mental arithmetic ☑

20. Struggle with mental arithmetic ☑

21. Learn multiplication facts, but then forget them overnight ☑

22. Only know the $2 \times$, $5 \times$ and $10 \times$ multiplication facts ☐

23. Count on to access the $2 \times$ and $5 \times$ facts ☐

24. Make 'big' errors for multiplication facts, such as $6 \times 7 = 67$ or $6 \times 7 = 13$ ☑

25. Like to use formulas, but uses them mechanically without any understanding of how they work ☐

26. Forget mathematical procedures, especially as they become more complex, such as decomposing or borrowing for subtraction and, almost certainly, the 'traditional' method for division ☑

27. Get very anxious about doing any mathematics ☑

28. Refuse to try any mathematics, especially unfamiliar topics ☑

29. Become impulsive when doing mathematics, rather than being analytical, rushing to get it over with? ☐

30. Show an inability to 'see' patterns or generalisations, especially ones that are incompatible with previous patterns, for example, seeing that 1/2, 1/3, 1/4, 1/5 is a sequence that is getting smaller ☑

31. Think that algebra is impossible to understand ☐

Using the Checklist

The Checklist can be used in a number of ways. It can be completed by the person being assessed, or by a teacher or a parent. If more than one list is collected then the responses can be compared. Each item can be ticked or left blank, or each item can be graded on a 1–3 scale:

1 Not a problem 2 Sometimes a problem 3 Always a problem

The Checklist can be filled in before the assessment and then individual items can be discussed during the assessment, maybe as a low stress introductory activity.

The responses will highlight areas of concern and could help in the construction of an intervention plan.

The responses from the Checklist can be compared to the responses from other tests for confirmation or flagged up for further investigation.

Note that there is no score that defines 'dyscalculia'. Obviously, if every item is scored as 'Always a problem' then that would be compelling evidence for such an inference.

4 Starting the assessment/diagnosis: Getting to know the person through informal activities

One of the goals of the assessment/diagnosis is to obtain the maximum performance for the subject, or at least a performance that is not significantly affected by anxiety and stress. The informal diagnostic activities described below should be low stress and should enable the tester to establish a relaxed and purposeful relationship with the subject. The goal, as ever, is to collect information as empathetically, accurately and efficiently as possible.

Being a set of informal tests, these activities need to be interpreted clinically. There are interpretations provided for all of the activities, but the individuality of people means that many reactions will be observed that are not covered in this book. That is where experience helps, but also where experience continues to grow, no matter how many assessments you have done.

I like to provide a selection of pens, pencils and pencils with eraser tops so that the subject can chose which they prefer to use.

Some informal starter questions

- How would you rate yourself in mathematics on a scale of 1 to 10?
- Which topics/bits in mathematics are you best at doing?
- Where about would you place yourself in terms of the others in your class?
- Are there any topics in mathematics where you might like some extra help?
- What are your worst topics in mathematics? Which ones do you like the least? (*Are they the same?*)
- How good are you at telling the time?
- How good are you with working out your money when you are shopping?

Informal diagnostic activities

These make good warm up questions for an individual assessment diagnosis as they are relatively low stress.

Activity 1. Estimating how many coins

Spread about 30 or 40 one pence coins or matches on a table and ask the subject to estimate the number, how many are there. Then ask him to count them.

The estimation part of this exercise gives you some idea about the subject's sense of number.

The counting checks one-to-one correspondence. Also it is of interest to see how the subject counts. Does he simply count one by one or does he arrange or pile the coins in fives or tens or use some grouping of numbers?

An estimate is not 'right' or wrong', so it is less open to judgment.

This activity gives you a sense of the subject's sense of a bigger quantity than used in the dots activity (2). It is a tactile activity, hands-on, so no symbols and, hopefully, low stress.

You could ask the subject to check their count and see if a different procedure is used. Is there any flexibility? You could ask, 'Can you count the coins by a different method?' if the flexibility is not spontaneous.

Activity 2. Recognising quantity/subitising/enumeration and sense of number

One of the (two) pre-requisite skills that Butterworth (2003) includes in his Dyscalculia Screener is the test of subitising, that is, the ability to enumerate a number of randomly arranged dots. It seems reasonable to consider that this skill must be a foundation for establishing a sense of number values. For small numbers of dots, say up to four dots, most people can just 'know' that there are four dots. Beyond this number they may have to hold the dot arrangement in their visual memory and count the dots in their mind, using their working memory. This may take the number of dots enumerated up to around seven. The process of visualising and counting extends the time used for reaching an answer.

This skill requires that the person has a firm connection in mind between the quantity of dots and the number name and symbol that labels that quantity. In other words they have to know that a group of four dots is called 'four' and is written as '4'. It may be that the person can recognise that, for example, a cluster of five dots is 'more dots' than a cluster of three dots without being able to give names to the clusters. One of the very useful, and low stress, questions that instructors can use with learners is, 'Is the answer bigger or smaller?' The question is about comparing number values and quantities.

It is the ability to progress from counting on (and back) in ones that takes the learner forward in understanding mathematics. Being stuck in these two stages is a sure sign of low developmental progress. An over-reliance on counting in ones will severely handicap progression in mathematics and will also handicap any development of number sense and the skill of estimation (see Chapter 11). Counting is where arithmetic begins. It is important, but as an early stage, not as a permanent strategy.

The activity

Show the test cards 1 to 6, each for about 1 second, each time asking, 'How many dots?'

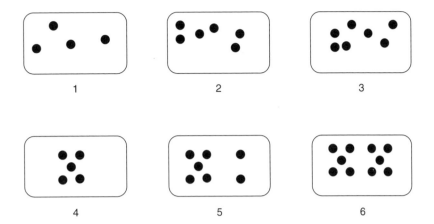

The activity looks at subitising skills with cards 1 to 3 and the ability to recognise patterns with cards 4 to 6. The diagnostic questions are:

1 Can the subject accurately recognise the number of randomly organised dots on cards 1–3? If the subject cannot recognise four dots, show four fingers, briefly (one second) and ask, 'How many fingers?'
2 Ask how he knew the number. Did he 'Just know' or did he visualise in working memory and count?'

If this task is not performed well, show cards 2 and 3 together for a brief time (1 second) and ask, 'Which card has more dots?' This will give some further evidence about the ability to understand quantity, but at a comparison level rather than absolute quantity. This may suggest a starting point for building early numbers skills, that is, start with work on 'bigger and smaller' (and use 'more' or 'less' for flexible vocabulary).

Did the performance improve for cards 4–6 where a pattern is involved? Do patterns help number sense? Are the numbers of dots on the three cards related to each other by the subject? Does he see that card 5 is 5 + 2 or that card 6 is 5 + 5 = 10?

This activity also looks at one-to-one correspondence in a situation where the objects can only be touched, not moved, so an element of tracking is involved. Does the subject touch the dots or eye-track? This will tell you about the level of counting ability. For example, is it still at the kinaesthetic stage or is the subject able to count in her head? Can she count accurately?

Activity 3. Counting 'in your head'

- Ask the subject to count in ones. Stop them at 25 (or sooner if struggling with the task).
- Ask them to count back from 25 (or 10 if 25 seems to create anxiety),
- Ask them to count in twos, starting at 2 and then at 1. Can they count backwards in twos?
- Ask them to count in tens, starting at zero and then at 7. Can they count backwards in tens?

The ability to count backwards may require working memory until it is automatised. Also the ability to count backwards in twos and tens is indicative of the ability to move on from ones in a skill that is a pre-requisite for subtraction.

Counting beyond 10 requires the learner to absorb inconsistencies in vocabulary. Eleven and twelve are exceptions and the teen vocabulary is in reverse order to the digits. Thus there is no verbal pattern and the task is about memory. Fortunately most people get so much exposure to this collection of numbers that recall is not a problem. However, the recall may disguise a lack of understanding of place value.

Knowing the numbers that are one more and one less than a tens number shows that the subject does not have to count up or back to achieve an answer and that they can deal with numbers that are close to tens (a pre-requisite skill for rounding up and rounding down).

Activity 4. Tens and units with coins

Give the subject about 23 1p coins and three or four 10p coins. Ask him to give you 9p. If he gives you nine one pence coins ask for another 9p and then again.

The subject does not have enough penny coins for the third 9p so does he offer a 10p and ask for change? Does he ask you to change a 10p coin for ten one pence coins? Does he say he can't because he doesn't have 9 one pence coins. You are exploring his sense of units and tens and crossing tens in terms of a familiar material, money, and thus the foundation of place value and a tendency to be numerically literal.

The activity could be extended by replacing the 1p and 10p coins with 10p and £1 coins.

This activity may also reveal an uncertainty with coinage.

Activity 5. Sharing and division

Give the subject 24 1p coins. Ask him to share them equally between two people. Then between four people.

How is the sharing done? One by one? Does he count the total, divide by two mentally and then count out 12? Does he group the coins in 5s or 10s. When you ask him to share between four people, does he start again with the 24 or does he half the groups of 12?

The activity links division to subtraction and investigates reliance on counting in another context.

Activity 6. Basic facts 1

(See Chapter 6 for norm-referenced tests for basic facts.)

Show some simple addition questions, each on a separate card.

$4 + 3 = ?$ used to check for accuracy and method.

Check for accuracy and strategy. Is the answer achieved by retrieval or counting or linking to 3 + 3 or 4 + 4?

3 + 8 = ?

An item that checks if the method used is to add 8 onto 3 or 3 onto 8. Is the task overviewed first?

Activity 7. Number bonds for 10

For younger subjects, place 10 1p coins on the table. Split them as 5 and 5 (in a line). Write 5 + 5 = 10 on paper. Ask the pupil to write other pairs of numbers that add to 10. Tell him he may use the coins to help if he wishes.

You are observing if he needs the coins or whether he can just work with the written digits. (And you can question him to make sure he is not just using the coins to humour you.) You are also observing how he organises this 'number bonds for 10' task. Is he random? Does he just do half the facts (that is 6 + 4, 7 + 3 ... and not recognise the commutative facts 4 + 6, 3 + 7 ...)? The exercise extracts information about these key facts in a somewhat less stressful manner and in a way that gives some hint as to underlying understanding of the pattern involved.

For older subjects, ask them to write two numbers that add up to make 10. If they are correct, ask them to write two more and so on until they are finished. What pair of numbers do they write first? Are they the key fact 5 + 5?

Activity 8. Basic facts 2

5 + 6 = ?

Ask how the answer was obtained. Is 5 + 6 interrelated to the 5 + 5 or to 6 + 6? You could also try 7 + 8 = ? to check if the double facts are used routinely.

4 + □ = 10

to investigate if the subject knows how to approach number bonds when written in a different format. This card could be followed by

10 + w = 18 for older learners to investigate links to algebra.

What number value is w?

13 − 7 = ?

To investigate subtraction skills. Do they count back? Or use 10 as a middle stage? Or doubles (14 = 7 + 7)?

It is possible to check recall of and strategies for addition and subtraction facts informally by simply asking the answers to a few random questions. It is worth asking how the subject knows the answer (recall or strategy). It should be interesting to compare recall of addition facts with recall of subtraction facts (which may indicate the level of confidence with which these facts are known). Watch for subtle counting techniques, such as counting objects in the room (eye movements give this away) or almost imperceptible movements of fingers resting on their leg. Less subtle are the pupils who tap their nose or chin as they count, which is truly an early stage of developing number skills.

Activity 9. Place value

Not only is the place value system a sophisticated and fundamental concept, it demands sequencing skills, directional skills, skills with symbols, including the interrelationship between numbers represented by words and numbers represented by symbols and an adequate short-term memory.

Central to understanding place value is the concept of zero, again a sophisticated concept, so we should not be too surprised if zero creates some difficulties for learners.

Writing numbers beyond nine takes the learner into the concept of place value. It also takes the learner to 'crossing the tens' and back again when counting backwards. These processes are essential pre-requisites for addition and subtraction, the next stage that children meet when learning mathematics.

For our everyday number system we use base 10 and place value. Place value means what it says, but maybe it doesn't say it clearly enough, for some learners, in just those two words.

When we write a number such as 34567, each digit has a numerical *value* which is dependent on the *place* it holds in the sequence. If we start with the smallest place value, the units, then we start on the right. The place values increase as we move left. This is the opposite direction to the one we use for reading a sentence or a word. This is an inconsistency, especially for those children who absorbed the sequence, 1, 2, 3, 4, 5, 6, 7, 8, 9, where the numbers increased in value from left to right and then do not have the flexibility of thinking to deal with the direction of the new sequence. (For more on the role of consistency in learning mathematics, see the companion volume to this book, *The Trouble with Maths* [Chinn, 2012: ch. 8].)

The activity

Use a series of place value cards to ask what specific digits represent, 'What is the value of this digit (or use 'number') in this place?' An extension is to try asking what happens to a digit when the number is multiplied or divided by 10, 100 or 1000 to check a deeper understanding of place value. Use of these cards requires a responsive flexibility from the tester.

Show each card and say:

Card 1. 'This number is nine hundred and seventy-one.'
Card 2 and ask, 'What is this number?'
Card 2 again, point to the 6 and say, 'The digit 6 has a value of six hundred.'
Card 3, point to the 1 and ask, 'What is the value of this digit?'
Or point to the 7 and say, 'What is the value of this digit?'
Card 4 and ask, 'What is this number?'
Card 3 again, point to the 8 and ask, 'What is the value of this digit?'
Card 5, point to the 5 and ask, 'What is the value of this digit?'
Card 6 and ask, 'What is this number?' What is the value of the 2?'

This activity can be based solely on symbols, for example, 'In the number 81673, what is the place value of the 6?' or based on materials, for example, 'When you look at these base 10 materials (Dienes blocks), show me the thousands.' Of course, the second activity requires some experience of base 10 materials in addition to an understanding of place value and indeed both need an understanding of what the term 'place value' means.

Two extension questions that could be used are 'What is the smallest number I could add to 98 to make a three digit number?' or 'What is the largest three digit number?'

And the sequential questions:

$14 \times 2 = ?$
$14 \times 20 = ?$
$14 \times 200 = ?$

Activity 10. Times table facts

'How are you getting on with knowing the times table facts? Which facts do you reckon you know really well? Can I ask you a couple of (those) facts?'

There are tests for basic facts in Chapter 6, but these only have norm-referenced data for ages 7 to 15, so these questions are useful for older subjects. Also they may provide enough information in some situations.

Activity 11. Putting numbers in order

For older subjects, 'Place these cards in order of value.'

| 0.1 | 0.012 | 0.02 | 0.0124 |

Other activities

This is not intended to be the definitive list of activities. More can and should be added and, of course, it is not necessary to use every activity every time. Build your own resources for you own circumstances.

As ever, there are clinical judgments to make.

Finally, don't forget the obvious

- Can they see? When looking at a book and/or the board?
- Can they hear? For example, can they hear the difference between, 'Three hundred' and 'Three hundredths' when said normally? Or fifteen and fifty?
- Does a coloured overlay make a difference?

Sometimes people do not know that they have a problem with seeing or hearing. They usually have no 'normal' experience to compare themselves with. It may not be that they can't see well, but it may be that the print on a page is not clear, or appears to move and therefore reading is tiring and stressful. Similar letters, numbers and shapes may be confused. They may have a problem with colours.

Poor vision or poor hearing may create predictable outcomes in the abilities to see and hear, but they may also have a detrimental effect on levels of concentration and application.

Colour blindness is more common in men than women. About 1 in 20 men have a problem whereas for women it is only 1 in 200. The most common form of colour blindness is confusing red and green. This problem does not usually affect the ability to do mathematics, but the use of colour in books and worksheets may be helpful for some learners and not for others.

Scotopic sensitivity. Irlen-Meares Syndrome

Scotopic sensitivity is also to do with colour, or to be more precise, to do with the contrast between print colour and paper colour when reading. It is also known as Irlen Syndrome or Irlen-Meares Syndrome. For some people the use of black print on white paper causes the print to blur or move. The problem also causes difficulties with sustained reading and with concentration levels. As with many difficulties the impact of the problem will be a spectrum. This makes it difficult to say how many people are affected, but it is thought to be about 10 per cent.

Although this section is titled 'Don't forget the obvious' people with the syndrome may not realise that they do have a problem. If their only experience in life is print that moves, they may think that is the norm for others, too. Standard eye tests from opticians are unlikely to pick up the problem. However, it is very easy for schools, employers and individuals to screen for the problem.

There seems to be no research about the effects of scotopic sensitivity syndrome on mathematics performance. However, there are implications that can be inferred. One of the symptoms is that the syndrome makes it more difficult to keep track of your place on a page. This must create problems for a learner trying to copy from a page of arithmetic or algebra examples. If this is combined with a poor short-term memory, then the problems may be very significant for the learner. A similarly significant problem is limited focusing. For some people with scotopic sensitivity, only a small number of letters, or digits, can be seen clearly. Again, research is not available, but it could well impact on reading multi-digit numbers or complex formulae.

It is possible to acquire coloured acetate overlays (for example, from Crossbow Education) and check if using these make any difference. It is also possible to print out some sample work on off-white paper, or coloured paper or to print work in a coloured font as a trial.

Other subtle problems with vision may need attention from a behavioural optometrist. For more information contact BABO (the British Association of Behavioural Optometrists).

The presentation of any worksheet or text book will also be a factor for some learners. Again the research is minimal, though a classroom study from Malta suggests that presentations that are too busy or too fussy can depress performance levels. It may be interesting and informative to take a fussy worksheet or page from a workbook and represent the information in a non-cluttered way and then compare scores.

The questions and activities in this chapter are designed to gather information, but also to set a relaxed, but purposeful tone for the assessment.

A record/observation sheet: informal items

Name _____

DoB _____ Date _____

How would you rate yourself in mathematics on a 1 to 10 scale?

Which topics/bits in mathematics are you best at doing?

Where about would you place yourself in terms of the others in your class?

Are there any topics in mathematics where you might like some extra help?

What are your worst topics in mathematics? Which ones do you like the least?

How good are you at telling the time?

How good are you with working out your money when you are shopping?

Activity 1. Estimating how many coins

Estimate: _____   Count: _____
Observations:

Activity 2. Recognising quantity/subitising/enumeration and sense of number

How many dots?
Card   1. _____   2. _____   3. _____   4. _____   5. _____   6. _____
Cards 2 and 3   More?

Card _____

Activity 3. Counting

Count in ones.

Count back from 25

Count in twos, starting at 2

Count in twos, starting at 1

Count backwards in twos

Count in tens, starting at zero and then at 7

Count backwards in tens?

Activity 4. Tens and units with coins

Activity 5. Sharing and division

Activity 6. Basic facts 1

$4 + 3 = ?$

$3 + 8 = ?$

Activity 7. Number bonds for 10

Activity 8. Basic facts 2

$5 + 6 = ?$

$4 + \square = 10$

$10 + w = 18$

$13 - 7 = ?$

Activity 9. Place value

Card 2. 'What is this number?'

Card 3. 'What is the value of this digit?' (1) or (7)

Card 4. 'What is this number?'

Card 3. 'What is the value of this digit?' (8)

Card 5. 'What is the value of this digit?' (.5)

Card 6. 'What is this number?' What is the value of the 2?

What is the smallest number I could I add to 98 to make a three digit number?'

'What is the largest three digit number?'

Card 7. 14 x 2 = ?

Card 8. 14 x 20 = ?

Card 9. 14 x 200 = ?

Activity 10. Putting numbers in order

Put these cards in order of the size of the numbers, biggest value number first, smallest last.

0.1   0.12   0.02   0.124

The Cards

Activity 2. How many dots?

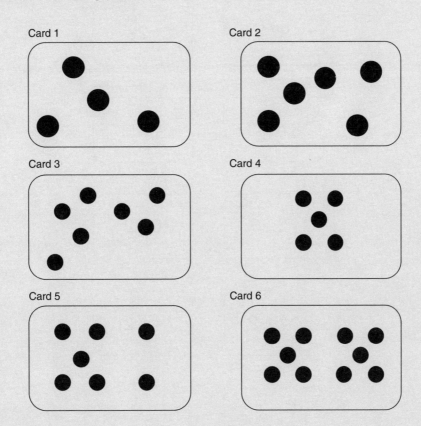

Card 1

Card 2

Card 3

Card 4

Card 5

Card 6

Activity 6. Basic facts 1

| 4 + 3 |

| 3 + 8 |

Activity 8. Number facts

| 5 + 6 |

| 4 + ☐ |

| 10 + w |

| 12 − 7 |

Activity 9. Place value

Card 1

971

Card 2

628

Card 3

81673

Card 4

4005

Card 5

72.53

Card 6

0.02

Card 7

14 x 2

Card 8

14 x 20

Card 9

14 x 200

Activity 11. Putting numbers in order

0.1

0.012

0.02

0.0124

5 Short-term memory and working memory: Two key underlying skills that influence learning

Working memory has been shown to be a significant predictor of mathematical achievement.

(Keeler and Swanson, 2001: 433)

The errors in mental calculations that will result from the loss of information in working memory will inevitably provide very poor conditions for the child to acquire number knowledge and rules.

(Gathercole and Alloway, 2008: 54)

One of the key goals of the test protocol advocated by this book is that each test or task that is included is testing factors that are relevant to learning. Short-term and working memory are key factors in many aspects of mathematics learning.

Short-term memory deals with information that is only required for a short time, for example, remembering a phone number while you key it into a phone, remembering the page number and exercise number the teacher has just announced, or remembering the mental arithmetic question you have just been asked to solve.

Working memory is used to process information mentally. The capacity of that working memory will control the complexity of the processing that can be successfully attempted.

Neither of these memories store information. The consequence is that, once forgotten, information cannot be recovered. This seems to me to be an important factor to consider when communicating with another person.

If teaching is to be efficacious then teachers and tutors need to know the short-term and working memory capacity of their students. In particular, teachers and tutors need to know the students whose short-term and working memories are weak. Short-term memory is a critical factor in communication. For example, if too much information, an amount that is beyond the short-term memory capacity of the individual, is presented, then the learner will not be able to remember some, or possibly all, of that information.

Although these memories influence many aspects of mathematics, it is mental arithmetic that absolutely requires an effective working memory in order for calculations to be performed 'in your head'. Thus, a good ability for mental arithmetic may be as much about working memory as it is about number skills. (See also Chapter 10 on thinking style.)

There is also an impact, a less dramatic one perhaps, on written arithmetic. Using an effective working memory while performing computations will make the process quicker partly because less documentation, for example tallies, is needed. Once again there is an interaction between the demands of the curriculum (or the culture of mathematics) and the characteristics of the learner. Teachers often expect students to work quickly in mathematics. Some students cannot and many would rather not (see also Chapter 7 on anxiety). In their survey of teacher identified characteristics in children who have mathematics learning difficulties (Bryant et al., 2000) 'Takes a long time to complete calculations' came sixth (out of 33).

The UK culture of including mental arithmetic tasks at the start of mathematics lessons and the assumption that mental arithmetic automatically improves mathematics achievement levels is not necessarily true for all students. (Indeed any assumption applied to *all* students is likely to be untrue.) It is obvious that any demand built into the curriculum affects the amount of success that learners experience and thus their motivation. However, teachers should be able to ameliorate much of the negative impact for those learners who may be disadvantaged by demands that are inappropriate for them by suitable and empathetic differentiation.

The simplest test for short-term and working memory is based on repeating a string of digits. This type of test is part of the WISC, the Wechsler Intelligence Scale for Children. Since this and other working memory tests are available elsewhere (for example, the Working Memory Rating Scale, Gathercole et al. [2008] or the Children's Memory Scale [Cohen, 1997]) the test included in this chapter is not a norm-referenced test.

The digit span tests are included to give a raw score measure of short-term and working memory capacities and particularly to identify those who have weak performances in these skills.

The tests

It should be noted that the tests ask the subject to perform the memory tasks in isolation, not in context, say for example, within a mental arithmetic question. The subject can focus all of their attention on the task. This is likely to give the optimum performance. There may well be some negative influence on performance when dual tasking, for example, using short-term memory to remember a question while beginning to calculate an answer.

Also in some situations there may be the influence of anxiety effecting performance. There is research that suggests that anxiety has a negative impact on working memory (Ashcraft et al., 1998).

The test as presented here is about screening for learners who are at risk from weak short-term and working memories. It is about a level of performance rather than a comparative, norm-referenced score.

Giving the test

It may be appropriate to explain the purpose of the test, that is, to find out how many items of information can be remembered and worked on mentally, by using two tasks.

Short-term memory test: Digits Forward (DF)

Name _____ Date _____

DF		response		response		response
2	85		16		29	
3	374		591		472	
4	7295		5183		3947	
5	58274		63859		85149	
6	362915		483962		274916	
7	8514739		5836192		1957263	
8	16952738		69152847		63859172	

Observations:

Working memory test: Digits Reversed (DR)

Name _____ Date _____

DR		response		response		response
2	62		38		74	
3	195		273		914	
4	4962		7361		8195	
5	39481		95816		14725	
6	725816		149583		691738	
7	7281594		9527183		3915827	
8	94184726		84273914		17495283	

Observations:

Short-term memory

Short term memory is measured by the tester saying, at one second intervals, a string of digits. When that information has been presented, the subject has to repeat them back to the tester. Give one practice example and then start with two digits forward. Allow for two presentations (there are three examples for each string of digits) to fail before stopping the test.

Always write down the response, whether correct or incorrect, so that the subject does not pick up clues as to their performance as they progress through the test.

Working memory

Working memory is measured by the tester saying, at one second intervals, a string of digits. When that information has been presented, the subject has to repeat them back to the tester, *in reverse order*. Give one example for practice and then start with two digits. Allow for two presentations to fail (at a level) before stopping the test. Again write down all the answers.

Variations

Some variations in testing these skills, for example, the Visual, Aural Digit Span (VADS [Koppitz, 1977]) explore different modalities. An extension here could be to ask the subject to write down their responses. There are people who can do a task in their head, but cannot get that answer down on paper. Again the procedures have to be flexibly responsive to the subject.

Self-monitoring when teaching

Once the information is collected you will know what abilities your students have in these two skills. You will need to monitor the performance of the students who have weak working and short-term memories. You will also need to monitor your own performance by noting how much information you give out at one time. Do you regularly exceed the capacity of some of your learners? Can you modify this by writing the information or repeating it in smaller 'chunks'? Analyse how many steps are needed to solve a problem by the method you have explained. Are there too many for some students' working memory capacity?

This is a pertinent example of a pragmatic (and empathetic) response to an awareness of diagnostic information. There will be no purpose in diagnosing difficulties if there are no positive outcomes for the learner. It is differentiation.

Further reading

Gathercole, S. and Alloway, T.P. (2008) *Working Memory and Learning. A Practical Guide for Teachers*. London: SAGE.

Alloway, T.P. (2011) *Improving Working Memory*. London: SAGE.

6 Tests of basic facts – addition, subtraction, multiplication and division: Their role in maths learning difficulties and dyscalculia

Four tests are included, one for each of the four operations. The age range covered is from 7 to 15 years (though for 7 years only addition and subtraction are included). For test subjects above the age of 15 years, informal questions are suggested.

The tests are norm-referenced from a sample of 2058 children, from over 40 independent and state schools across the UK. The tests for addition and subtraction facts have a time limit of 60 seconds. The tests for multiplication and division facts have a time limit of 120 seconds. The interpretation and implications of the answers and scores are discussed.

What is a 'basic fact'?

In the UK these are the 121 addition and subtraction facts from 0 to 20 (0 + 0 to 10 + 10) and the 121 multiplication and division facts from 0 to 100 (0 × 0 to 10 × 10). Prior to decimalisation the basic facts would have also included facts for 11 and 12. Presumably the principle behind the drive to memorise and quickly retrieve these facts from memory is that they are the basic essential facts and that they can then be used in all future calculations and computations. In Chapter 5 of *The Trouble with Maths* (Chinn, 2012), I explain how a smaller collection of basic facts can be used to achieve the same objectives. This is an example of the interaction between what a learner can do and what the curriculum and pedagogy ask and expect and then whether there is enough awareness and flexibility to address any disparity.

For many of the traditional methods taught for computations in UK schools, for example, 'long division', 'the grid method' or 'Napier's bones', the ability to access these facts is an essential pre-requisite. But, being unable to access the facts can be a barrier to developing an understanding of many other maths concepts. At the simplest level it can mean that a child takes so much time trying to access the facts they have less practice with the computations and procedures and often get incorrect answers. At a second level, anxiety, de-motivation and helplessness are likely consequences. At a third level, much of the 'later' work in maths is based on the processes that underlie the concepts and structures behind these basic facts.

Research

The research on dyscalculia and on maths learning difficulties draws attention to the role played by poor retrieval of the basic facts for the four operations, addition, subtraction, multiplication and division. For example, Ramaa and Gowramma (2002), in a comprehensive review of the literature include:

A persistence of fact retrieval deficits throughout elementary school.

(Ostad, 1997)

Fact retrieval deficits attributed to deficiencies in speed of processing.

(Ackerman and Dykman, 1996)

A deficiency in two areas of mathematical cognition, namely retrieval of number facts and the ability to solve story problems.

(Russell and Ginsburg, 1984)

One of Geary's (2010) conclusions from a five-year longitudinal study into mathematical cognition deficits in children with learning and intellectual disabilities was that fact retrieval becomes more important across grades in mathematics.

However, poor retrieval of these facts is not just a characteristic of people who are identified as dyscalculic or as having maths learning difficulties. The problem is more widespread than that. I often ask the teachers who attend my training sessions in the UK what percentage of children at about 11-years-old do not 'know' the times table facts. The responses are usually that this is above 50 per cent of pupils. This seems to be the situation with adults, too. However, the problem is a little more complicated than that.

Devlin (2000) observed:

Despite many hours of practise most people encounter great difficulty with the multiplication tables. Discounting the one times table and the ten times table as presenting no difficulty, the entire collection of multiplication tables amounts to only 64 separate facts ... Most people have little problem with two times table or the five times table. Discounting their entries leaves just 36 single-digit multiplications ... In fact, anyone who remembers that you can swap the order in multiplication (for example, 4×7 is the same as 7×4) can cut the total in half, to 18 (p. 60).

Devlin compares this level of attainment to the typical vocabulary of 13,000 to 15,000 words for a child of 6 years.

At this stage, we do not know why people cannot succeed in rote learning these facts. We just know that they can't and simply saying that *they should learn them*, as some fundamentalists insist, will not solve the problem.

The role of basic facts in maths and maths education

Educators are becoming increasingly aware that children and adults use linking strategies to access facts that they cannot retrieve direct from memory, for example, Gersten et al. (2005):

Increasingly the term arithmetic (or number) combinations is used, because basic problems involving addition and subtraction can be solved in a variety of ways and are not always retrieved as 'facts' (p. 294).

A second example of this awareness is taken from the *Primary School Curriculum Document, Ireland* (1999):

> All children can gain from using strategies for number facts. They can learn the 'easy' facts first ($\times$ 1, $\times$ 2, $\times$ 5, $\times$ 10) and use these to build up others … these strategies are of particular help to children with memory problems.

Unfortunately, not all educators are aware that rote learning does not necessarily result in facts being retained in memory, for example a spokesman for the English maths curriculum, quoted from the *TES* in February 2006:

> Year 3 pupils (age 7 years) will be expected to learn the 3 $\times$ and 4 $\times$ tables (it was Year 4) 'It is not about drilling children in their tables, *but at some stage children do need to know them.*'

I am not sure that expectations or indeed necessity are enough to facilitate success in this task.

Of course, it depends on what is meant by 'know'. 'Know' could mean instant retrieval from memory or it could mean the ability to access a fact by linking it to other facts. The basic facts in maths have this benefit. It is possible to work them out by linking strategies. This is not true, of course, for many other facts in life. For example, if you cannot recall the name of the capital city of France. If you have forgotten that it is Paris, there is no way to work it out from any information about the capitals of other countries you may have in your memory. However, if you cannot recall the product, 6×6, you could derive the answer by one of a number of links, for example, 5×6 plus 6, or $3 \times 6 \times 2$.

A small scale study of children aged by Gray and Tall (1994) showed that the children who achieved well in maths used linking strategies to access the facts they did not remember, but the low achieving children did not. This may be another example of the chicken and egg conundrum. It may also have some implications for interpreting data from the diagnostic tests and procedures.

A further issue is that just because a child or adult 'knows' the facts, does not mean that they can use them. Children with a good long-term memory for basic facts may give the illusion of learning (Chinn, 2010). So, the results from these tests have to be interpreted alongside the results from other tests. A high score does not guarantee success in maths and a low score does not necessarily mean failure. This is another reason why this book contains a range of formal and informal tests covering the different facets of learning maths. And we must not forget that learning outcomes often depend on the curriculum and on how it is taught.

It seems sensible that teaching should be based on research into learning (see Hattie, 2009). Geary (2011) observed that there is now considerable scientific knowledge on learning and cognition that could be, but is not applied to improve student learning. One example of this research is from the National Research Council of the USA (Bransford et al., 2000). The NRC put forward three Key Findings on learning. Key Finding 2 is pertinent here:

To develop competence in an area of inquiry, students must:

1   have a deep foundation of factual knowledge,
2   understand facts and ideas in the context of a conceptual framework, and
3   organise knowledge in ways that facilitate retrieval and application.

Unfortunately, for many people and too many educators, the 'deep foundation of factual knowledge' implies that all of the basic number facts and basic algorithms should be retrievable from memory. They are less concerned about 'understanding the facts and procedures in the context of a conceptual framework' and equally unconcerned about 'organising the knowledge in ways that facilitate retrieval'.

To be specific for the basic number facts then, I suggest that we have to consider what constitutes a 'deep foundation of factual knowledge' for these facts. It might mean, in this case, certain key basic facts. Then what defines these facts as 'key' is that they are understood in a conceptual framework and used in ways that facilitate the retrieval and application of other facts. The 'extension' of key basic facts to access other facts is explained in detail in the second edition of *The Trouble with Maths* (Chinn, 2012: ch. 5). The strategies for accessing other facts are about understanding the facts and ideas within the context of a conceptual framework thus organising the knowledge of these key facts in ways that facilitate retrieval and application, that is, strategies based on Key Finding 2.

First, the relevance of the information obtained about accessing basic facts is not just about what facts the person can retrieve from memory, but about their ability to access the facts they cannot remember and the sophistication of the strategies used to achieve retrieval. Second, it is not just about mathematics as an intellectual exercise, but about the demands of the curriculum and how it is taught and the appropriateness of the pedagogy for the individual. Finally, a lack of ability to learn these facts may be the first experience of persistent failure for the child and thus one of the early contributors to de-motivation.

The basic fact tests

The tests presented in this chapter are similar in basic design to Westwood's (2000) tests. They are structured in this way to be less stressful than 'quick-fire' tests where a string of facts are presented, one fact after another, usually at short time intervals, say 3 seconds. 'Quick-fire' tests do not favour children and adults who are slow processors or those who have poor short-term and/or working memories. They may also create a debilitating anxiety such that the child or adult being tested gives up and withdraws from the test. By presenting the facts visually, all together on one sheet, one operation per sheet, the slow processors can work at their own speed and, hopefully, provide some answers. Without answers there is no information for any diagnosis! The time limits of 60 and 120 seconds are not designed to put the subjects under pressure, but simply to limit the time they have to spend on these four tests.

The tests present 36 facts each for addition, subtraction and multiplication, and 33 facts for division. The adult or child has 60 seconds to attempt the addition facts and then 60 seconds for the subtraction facts, 120 seconds to attempt the multiplication and then 120 seconds for the division facts. These times were decided upon after trials with students. Sixty seconds for the addition and subtraction facts was sufficient for the majority of students to demonstrate their knowledge. One hundred and twenty seconds worked better for the multiplication and division facts, primarily in the sense that it provided more information and created less stress.

If it is felt appropriate there can be breaks between the individual tests or after two tests.

As with all the tests in this book, the information extracted from the test will usually be greatly augmented by informal (clinical) questioning. This further information will most likely come from the questions, 'Can you tell me how you got that answer? How did you work it out?' These questions should be directed to answers that are correct as well as those that are incorrect. Also, watching the students as they work on the tests can provide extra information, for example, the items that need more time, the use of counting or sub-vocalising.

It may be appropriate to use informal questions about these facts at the start of the assessment/diagnostic session (Chapter 4) and use the tests later as a follow-up, or it may be that you consider these tests are inappropriate for that person. Such decisions are part of the skill of diagnosing. Instead of using the tests you may decide simply to ask informal questions such as, 'How do you manage with basic facts, for example, 7 + 6 and 4 × 9?' 'Which times table facts do you know well?' Again the skill is to know how to ask the question, when to ask it and to know whether the answer is a true reflection of reality.

(Note that ten of the items on the Dyscalculia Checklist are about basic facts.)

Using the basic fact tests: test procedure

The four tests should be given out, one at a time, each after the previous test has finished. The time for each test should be exact and used for the questions, not for writing name, date, etc. Although average scores and norm-referenced data are provided (on page 61–62), these should only be used as guidelines and not for absolute conclusions. Much depends on which strategies are used when retrieval fails. This leads to use of the ever-present diagnostic question, 'How did you get your answer?', which can be used after the tests are completed.

The data for norm-referencing these tests was collected using black print on white paper. Some children find a less severe contrast between print and paper colour easier to read. If black print on white paper creates a debilitating effect, then it is a pragmatic decision to offer coloured paper and/or print. Technically the test is not then being given under standardised conditions. This should be noted against the results recorded, preferably with the black on white scores included for comparison and as some indication of the efficacy of the change.

The test asks for date of birth and age. This may create difficulties for some children, for example, they may not be able to recall their year of birth. As the norm-referenced data is given for age as a year, not as year/month, this should not create any anxiety, but still ask for this information after the tests have been completed.

Pre-test instructions:

I would like you to try these four short tests on the basic facts of maths. I don't want to spend too much time on these facts, so we will use 60 seconds, one minute, for the addition facts and the same for the subtraction facts, for you to do as many as you can. **Work across and down the sheet.** For the multiplication facts and for the division facts we will use 120 seconds, two minutes, for you to try as many as you can. Again, **work across and down the sheet.**

When you have finished the tests, please write your name and age at the top of each of the sheets.

The 60 second test for addition

Name _____ **Date** _____ **Age** _____ (y) _____ (m)

$2 + 1 = $ ____	$2 + 2 = $ ____	$1 + 3 = $ ____
$5 + 2 = $ ____	$3 + 3 = $ ____	$2 + 4 = $ ____
$3 + 5 = $ ____	$5 + 5 = $ ____	$6 + 5 = $ ____
$6 + 4 = $ ____	$4 + 4 = $ ____	$5 + 4 = $ ____
$2 + 8 = $ ____	$9 + 1 = $ ____	$4 + 6 = $ ____
$3 + 7 = $ ____	$6 + 3 = $ ____	$6 + 6 = $ ____
$6 + 7 = $ ____	$2 + 7 = $ ____	$3 + 6 = $ ____
$5 + 7 = $ ____	$8 + 4 = $ ____	$4 + 9 = $ ____
$9 + 5 = $ ____	$7 + 6 = $ ____	$8 + 9 = $ ____
$9 + 8 = $ ____	$9 + 6 = $ ____	$8 + 8 = $ ____
$5 + 8 = $ ____	$8 + 7 = $ ____	$9 + 9 = $ ____
$7 + 8 = $ ____	$8 + 9 = $ ____	$7 + 7 = $ ____

Score _____ Average score for age group_____

The 60 second test for subtraction

Name _____ **Date** _____ **Age** _____ (y) _____ (m)

$2 - 1 =$ _____ $\qquad$ $4 - 1 =$ _____ $\qquad$ $4 - 2 =$ _____

$5 - 2 =$ _____ $\qquad$ $6 - 3 =$ _____ $\qquad$ $2 - 2 =$ _____

$5 - 4 =$ _____ $\qquad$ $7 - 2 =$ _____ $\qquad$ $6 - 5 =$ _____

$7 - 3 =$ _____ $\qquad$ $7 - 7 =$ _____ $\qquad$ $8 - 7 =$ _____

$8 - 6 =$ _____ $\qquad$ $8 - 4 =$ _____ $\qquad$ $7 - 4 =$ _____

$9 - 3 =$ _____ $\qquad$ $8 - 5 =$ _____ $\qquad$ $9 - 6 =$ _____

$10 - 5 =$ _____ $\qquad$ $10 - 3 =$ _____ $\qquad$ $10 - 7 =$ _____

$11 - 1 =$ _____ $\qquad$ $11 - 3 =$ _____ $\qquad$ $12 - 3 =$ _____

$13 - 3 =$ _____ $\qquad$ $12 - 6 =$ _____ $\qquad$ $11 - 5 =$ _____

$14 - 4 =$ _____ $\qquad$ $12 - 9 =$ _____ $\qquad$ $14 - 5 =$ _____

$15 - 8 =$ _____ $\qquad$ $16 - 9 =$ _____ $\qquad$ $16 - 8 =$ _____

$17 - 6 =$ _____ $\qquad$ $17 - 9 =$ _____ $\qquad$ $18 - 9 =$ _____

Score _____ Average score for age group _____

The 120 second test for multiplication

Name _____ **Date** _____ **Age** _____ (y) _____ (m)

$1 \times 2 =$ _____ $\qquad$ $2 \times 2 =$ _____ $\qquad$ $2 \times 5 =$ _____

$0 \times 3 =$ _____ $\qquad$ $3 \times 2 =$ _____ $\qquad$ $3 \times 3 =$ _____

$1 \times 8 =$ _____ $\qquad$ $6 \times 2 =$ _____ $\qquad$ $3 \times 4 =$ _____

$5 \times 3 =$ _____ $\qquad$ $7 \times 2 =$ _____ $\qquad$ $10 \times 2 =$ _____

$2 \times 8 =$ _____ $\qquad$ $8 \times 3 =$ _____ $\qquad$ $4 \times 5 =$ _____

$6 \times 4 =$ _____ $\qquad$ $3 \times 7 =$ _____ $\qquad$ $4 \times 10 =$ _____

$3 \times 9 =$ _____ $\qquad$ $9 \times 3 =$ _____ $\qquad$ $7 \times 0 =$ _____

$8 \times 4 =$ _____ $\qquad$ $5 \times 6 =$ _____ $\qquad$ $4 \times 8 =$ _____

$4 \times 7 =$ _____ $\qquad$ $7 \times 5 =$ _____ $\qquad$ $6 \times 6 =$ _____

$5 \times 9 =$ _____ $\qquad$ $10 \times 9 =$ _____ $\qquad$ $7 \times 7 =$ _____

$7 \times 9 =$ _____ $\qquad$ $6 \times 8 =$ _____ $\qquad$ $8 \times 8 =$ _____

$9 \times 9 =$ _____ $\qquad$ $8 \times 7 =$ _____ $\qquad$ $7 \times 6 =$ _____

Score _____ Average score for age group _____

The 120 second test for division

Name _____ Date_____ Age _____ (y) _____ (m)

$2 \div 1 =$ _____ $4 \div 1 =$ _____ $4 \div 2 =$ _____

$6 \div 2 =$ _____ $6 \div 3 =$ _____ $9 \div 3 =$ _____

$10 \div 2 =$ _____ $12 \div 4 =$ _____ $10 \div 5 =$ _____

$16 \div 4 =$ _____ $15 \div 3 =$ _____ $20 \div 5 =$ _____

$20 \div 4 =$ _____ $24 \div 4 =$ _____ $30 \div 3 =$ _____

$30 \div 5 =$ _____ $12 \div 6 =$ _____ $24 \div 6 =$ _____

$50 \div 5 =$ _____ $36 \div 4 =$ _____ $24 \div 8 =$ _____

$35 \div 5 =$ _____ $45 \div 5 =$ _____ $36 \div 6 =$ _____

$40 \div 8 =$ _____ $54 \div 6 =$ _____ $36 \div 9 =$ _____

$49 \div 7 =$ _____ $64 \div 8 =$ _____ $54 \div 9 =$ _____

$72 \div 8 =$ _____ $81 \div 9 =$ _____ $42 \div 7 =$ _____

Score _____ Average score for age group _____

The Data

Data for each operation is presented below. The average scores show a steady increase with age in almost every case. However, there is an interesting dip at age 11, the age at which most children transfer to secondary education. (See also the dip in scores for the 15 minute mathematics test.)

The standard deviations, a measure of the spread of the scores, are fairly consistent across the age range for each of the operations. 16 per cent of the pupils should have scores one standard deviation or more below the mean and 16 per cent should have scores one standard deviation or more above the mean.

The tables also include scores for the 25th, 10th and 5th percentile (sometimes rounded to the nearest whole number) so that these critical levels can be identified.

What the tests reveal

Although the raw scores from these tests will provide information about the comparative achievement level of knowing basic facts, there is the possibility of extracting more information about the strategies used to access these facts by using follow-up, clinical questions.

A good score may still need follow-up questions. Instant retrieval may not guarantee understanding. It may reflect hours of practising (and thus persistence). Sadly, it may not guarantee long-term retention. What we do not practise or 'top up' in our brain gets forgotten.

Strategies for accessing basic facts may include:

- counting on (for example, 7×2 accessed by counting 2, 4, 6, 8, 10, 12, 14) or
- linking facts (for example, 7×2 accessed in two steps, two partial products, 5×2 is 10, 2×2 is 4, $10 + 4$ is 14)

Understanding the concept of multiplication could be checked by asking a fact beyond the rote-learned collection, for example 15×8 and asking how the subject achieved their answer. The 'How did you get the answer?' question can be used to explore strategies.

If the subject can only use counting, especially counting in ones, to access the facts, then this suggests a low level of cognitive development. It also suggests a tendency to an inchworm thinking style of small forward steps (Chapter 10), rather than an awareness of patterns and links. It may well mean that work rates are slow.

If the subject uses linking strategies, for example computing $4 \times$ facts by doubling $2 \times$ facts or using 5×6 plus 2×6 to access 7×6, then this usually indicates an understanding of the procedures of multiplication and the interrelationships between numbers. This is usually a more positive indicator of potential success in mathematics.

The ability to understand and use linking strategies may enhance confidence and reduce the feelings of helplessness.

There is an argument that automatic retrieval of basic facts allows the learner to focus on procedures. Equally, there could be an argument that poor retrieval will handicap the learning of and application of procedures. This suggests that when new procedures are introduced to learners the basic facts used should be ones that are accessible and thus do not act as a barrier to learning a new concept. An alternative intervention is to provide an addition square and/or a multiplication fact square (and demonstrate how it is used).

It should be noted that even if a learner has high scores on these tests it does not guarantee high performance levels in maths. I assessed two teenage students in the same week who demonstrated accurate and quick recall division facts but could not solve the equation F = ma if the values for F and m were given. Fast and accurate retrieval of these facts may give (again) an illusion of learning. They are a body of facts that many parents are comfortable with and therefore they are happy to practise them with their children. Most other areas of maths receive far less attention. I suspect that very few parents practise fractions on the school run. Practice may 'make perfect', but it does not necessarily make for understanding and actually it may not always 'make perfect', otherwise we would all be world champions (and 'perfect' may not be the appropriate goal).

Finally, there is a possibility that a person may become de-skilled at the task of retrieving answers for basic facts. Young children practise these facts quite regularly, but this ceases to happen as children get older. I have known students with very poor recall of basic facts at age 15 years who still went on to achieve a top grade in GCSE mathematics. And, as one of my ex-students told me after he got his maths degree, 'They don't ask you what 8×7 is in the final year of a maths degree!' Conclusions should not be made from just one source of information.

Norm-referenced test scores

(2058 pupils from over 40 schools across the UK)

Addition (36 facts)

Age (years)	Average	SD	25 percentile score	10 percentile score	5 percentile score
7	11.8	5.7	7	5	4
8	17.4	6.4	12	9	8
9	21.6	7.2	17	12	9
10	24.4	7.3	20	15	11
11	23.6	7.6	19	13	10
12	24.6	7.4	21	15	11
13	27.6	7.6	22	18	14
14	29.9	6.6	25	20	18
15	28.8	7.7	24	18	15

Subtraction (36 facts)

Age (years)	Average	SD	25 percentile score	10 percentile score	5 percentile score
7	10.3	5.3	7	5	3
8	15.4	7.1	10	7	5
9	20.5	8.1	15	11	8
10	22.4	8.3	17	12	9
11	22.1	8.3	16	12	10
12	23.3	7.8	17	12	10
13	26.3	7.9	21	15	12
14	28.4	7.3	23	18	16
15	27.8	7.3	23	18	15

Multiplication (36 facts)

Age (years)	Average	SD	25 percentile score	10 percentile score	5 percentile score
7	(test not given)				
8	18.7	7.7	15	8	5
9	24.3	8.7	18	13	10
10	26.8	8.7	21	15	12
11	25.8	8.9	19	14	10
12	26.8	8.2	21	15	11
13	28.5	8.3	24	16	12
14	29.8	7.3	25	20	16
15	31.0	6.5	29	22	16

Division (33 facts)

Age (years)	Average	SD	25 percentile score	10 percentile score	5 percentile score
7	Test not given				
8	11.0	8.3	4	2	1
9	18.3	9.9	11	5	2
10	21.4	10.1	15	6	3
11	19.1	10.7	11	3	1
12	20.0	10.0	12	5	2
13	23.7	9.8	18	7	3
14	25.1	9.4	19	10	5
15	25.5	8.2	19	15	10

If a pupil scores in between these selected values, then some sensible interpolation should lead to a satisfactory estimate of the percentile for that score.

The positive approach is to find what is known and build on those facts, while remembering to continue to rehearse what is known. Link the diagnosis to the intervention.

7 Mathematics anxiety: Which topics and activities create anxiety?

Many people confess to being anxious about mathematics. It is socially acceptable in Western culture to admit to having low abilities with numbers, a strategy that often lowers mathematics anxiety in adults by lowering expectations. So, if expectations of ability can be forestalled, then poor performance and anxiety have less impact on self-esteem. This strategy does not always work and many people suffer from low self-esteem as a consequence of what they perceive as a personal failure.

Researchers have offered descriptions of mathematics anxiety, focusing on different causes and consequences, for example, it has been defined as 'feelings of tension, apprehension or fear that interfere with mathematics performance' (Richardson and Shuinn, 1972) or as 'a state of discomfort which occurs in response to situations involving mathematics tasks which are perceived as threatening to self-esteem' (Cemen quoted in Trujillo and Hadfield, 1999). Richardson and Shuinn focus on the impact of anxiety on cognitive performance while Cemen considers the impact on self-esteem, an affective issue. These two focuses illustrate the multi-faceted influence of anxiety on the ability to learn mathematics and on the confidence to learn mathematics.

The multi-faceted nature of anxiety was also noted by Datta and Scarfpin (1983) who identified two types of mathematics anxiety, which they described by the factors that cause them. One is caused by mental blocks in the process of learning mathematics and the other is a result of socio-cultural factors. Mental block anxiety may be initiated, for example, by a mathematics symbol or a concept that creates a barrier for the person learning mathematics. This could be the introduction in algebra of letters for numbers or the seemingly inexplicable procedure for long division or failing to memorise the 'basic' multiplication facts. This type of mathematics anxiety may be addressed by appropriate teaching, if the mathematics curriculum allows for this, both in time and in structure.

Ashcraft et al. (1998) have shown that, under certain circumstances, anxiety can adversely affect the working memory that is used for mathematical tasks. Working memory has been shown to be a significant predictor of mathematical achievement (Keeler and Swanson, 2001). Thus anxiety does not just block the willingness to learn, it can also reduce the capacity of one of the key sub-skills needed to succeed (see also Chapter 5).

Socio-cultural mathematics anxiety is a consequence of the common beliefs about mathematics such as; 'only very clever (and slightly strange) people can do mathematics' or that 'there is only ever one right answer to a problem' (thus it is very judgmental) or 'if you cannot learn the basic facts you will never be any good at mathematics'. This type of mathematics anxiety may well lead to mathematics phobia, but it also sanctions people to admit in social situations that they are unable to do mathematics.

Hadfield and McNeil (1994) suggest that there are three causes of mathematics anxiety, environmental, intellectual and personality. Environmental anxiety includes classroom issues, parental pressure and the perception of mathematics as a rigid set of rules. Intellectual anxiety includes a mismatch of learning styles and teaching styles (see also Chapter 10) and self-doubt and personality factors include a reluctance to ask questions in class and low self-esteem. From my experience as a teacher I consider this 'triple causes' construct to be realistic in that it considers many, often interrelated factors. The anxiety questionnaire used in this chapter was structured to reflect these factors.

Mathematics anxiety can impact on many aspects of learning, for example, in a classroom study (Chinn, 1995) comparing the errors made in basic computation by dyslexic and non-dyslexic students, the error patterns and frequency of particular errors were not different in the two groups with one notable exception, the error of 'no attempt'. Although this error occurred with both groups, the frequency of this error was much higher within the dyslexic group.

This behaviour avoids failure. The fear of failure exacerbates feelings of anxiety. All learning involves taking risks, but the extremely judgmental nature of mathematics intensifies the sense of risk and thus can soon discourage children from being involved in mathematics tasks. There was ample evidence of this 'error' in use in the (over 2500) scripts used to provide data to make the 15 minute mathematics test a norm-referenced test (Chapter 8).

Lundberg and Sterner (2006) commented on the importance of being aware of the affective factors on learning mathematics:

> however, over and above the common cognitive demands and neurological representations and functions, performance in reading and arithmetic is influenced by a number of motivational and emotional factors such as need of achievement, task orientation, helplessness, depression, anxiety, self-esteem, self-concept, locus of control ...

Two consequences of the impact of mathematics anxiety on the processes of learning mathematics were noted by Skemp (1986). He observed that the reflective activity of intelligence is most easily inhibited by anxiety. Skemp (1971) also explained how an over-reliance on rote learning as a dominant culture in mathematics may lead to anxiety and loss of self-esteem for many pupils. Unfortunately, 35 years later a 2006 report shows that little has changed in England with the culture of mathematics education. 'Evaluation of mathematics provision for 14–19 year olds' a report by Ofsted, the English Government school inspection body, noted that, 'Mathematics became an apparently endless series of algorithms for them (*students*), rather than a coherent and inter-connected body of knowledge.'

Mathematics is a unique subject in the school curriculum in that most of the questions that pupils have to answer have only one correct answer. Mathematics in schools is thus inherently judgmental in that answers are either right or they are wrong. This situation, combined with many other factors, such as an unsuitable curriculum, the culture of doing mathematics quickly, the over-reliance on rote learning, can lead pupils towards a negative attributional style (Chinn, 2004; Chinn and Ashcroft, 2007) and ultimately learned helplessness (Seligman, 1998).

It could be claimed that the culture of speed and absolute accuracy conflicts with the confidence that has to be nurtured to develop estimation skills or problem solving skills.

Mathematics helplessness can, not surprisingly, persist into adulthood. For example, Zaslavsky (1999) looked at over 200 mathematics 'autobiographies' from mathematics anxious people in the USA. She observed a common thread. The respondents felt powerless, out of control and lacking in self-esteem.

There is a concern that mathematics abilities in the adult population of the UK are unacceptably low (Confederation of British Industry, 2006). Anxiety will be one of the contributing factors to the situation where approximately 50 per cent of the adult population cannot do mathematics at a level beyond that they were taught when aged 11.

The mathematics anxiety questionnaire in this chapter looks at the anxiety levels of students in secondary education, which is the stage in education where students approach adulthood and a stage when many children reach their 'mathematical limit'.

There may well be a connection between significantly low achievement in mathematics and anxiety. For example, if mathematics anxiety reached a level at which the student withdrew from any future learning and this occurred early in his schooling, then he may well present with seriously low mathematics achievement levels. A contributing factor to this scenario could be a mismatch between the learner and the instruction he receives, hence the inclusion of a chapter on thinking (cognitive) styles in this book.

In a small study Chinn (1996) looked at the relationship between WISC scores and the grades achieved in GCSE mathematics by dyslexic pupils at a specialist school. Although the correlations between the various sub-scores and mathematics grades were interesting, a key, informal outcome came from the results for the average band of students where affective factors played the dominant role. Although I had no standardised measure of these factors I was well aware of individual attitudes, motivation and anxiety from my weekly experience of teaching each student for at least one of their mathematics lessons.

I suggest that some measure, or at least some investigation, of anxiety should be a part of any diagnostic protocol for mathematics learning difficulties and dyscalculia.

One set of data for the anxiety questionnaire in this chapter came from the responses from 442 dyslexic male students, provided by nine schools from the Specialist Provision and Special Unit categories of CReSTeD (Council for the Registration of Schools Teaching Dyslexic Students). There were not enough responses from female dyslexic students to make a viable sample.

A further set of responses came from 2084 mainstream students, provided by 19 schools from around England. Five of these schools were independent. The sample was taken from Years 7 to 11. Students enter secondary education in Year 7 at age 11 and will be 16 at the end of Year 11. The schools were selected to provide a geographical spread across England.

The mathematics anxiety questionnaire

The questionnaire is a mixture of items focusing on different activities which might cause anxiety. For example, some items refer directly to specific tasks in mathematics, such as long division. Others relate to classroom activities, such as mental arithmetic, others to the culture of mathematics, such as having to do mathematics questions quickly, and others to social aspects, such as showing a mathematics report to Mum or Dad. As English education is currently in the grip of almost obsessive levels of testing, the questionnaire includes items related to this all too frequent experience.

However, to balance this opinion, one of the conclusions from the National (US) Mathematics Advisory Board's study on learning mathematics was that testing aids learning by requiring the recall of content relevant information.

The students' grades for the anxiety caused by each item, using a Likert scale of 1–4, where 1 is 'never anxious' and 4 is 'always anxious' are, obviously, entirely subjective.

The questionnaires were presented and read to the students by teachers in each of the participating schools. The results were analysed as 15 groups: males and females for each of the five year groups and male dyslexic students for each year group.

The average 'score' was calculated for each item for each group. The 20 items from the questionnaire were then ranked for each group.

The maximum possible score on the questionnaire is 80. The minimum possible score is 20. On the basis that a rating of the 'often' anxiety level was 3 and that there are 20 items, the percentages of students scoring at 60 and above were calculated for each group to provide an indication the prevalence of high levels of anxiety.

The group showing the greatest anxiety as measured by the 'high anxiety scores' (>59) were Year 7 dyslexic males. The percentage of high anxiety scores for dyslexic students then decreased, with a slight increase in Year 11. There was an increase in high anxiety scores (>59) for females in Year 11 with values higher than those for the males. Year 11 is the GCSE (National) examination year in England.

Scores on this questionnaire are not absolute. They could be influenced, whether as a total, or in the ranking of an individual Item, by many factors. Empathetic discussion with the subject may reveal these influences.

Also, an individual score on the questionnaire may not reflect the true levels of anxiety in every student, for example, a Year 8 female scored a close-to-average total of 45, but wrote on her questionnaire, 'I hate mathematics. I can never do it. If I'm with the right teacher, then I can do it easily, but I cannot.' Again we have to remember that the scores are, inevitably, subjective.

The scores for high anxiety in mathematics show that between 2 and 6 per cent of mainstream students experience high levels of anxiety about mathematics, at a level that suggests they are 'often' anxious. Dyslexic males do not consistently show greater percentages of high anxiety across the year groups, but the comparatively high percentage in Year 7 is notable. A possible hypothesis is that Year 7 could be their first year in specialist education and the benefits of specialist provision have yet to take affect.

Reflections on the scores from the questionnaire

The responses to the questionnaire could almost be considered as a reflection of pupils' experiences of mathematics or consumer feedback on mathematics, the mathematics curriculum and the mathematics culture that exist in England.

There are more similarities between the groups than there are differences. However, females tended to score with slightly higher levels of anxiety than males and dyslexic males tended to score with higher levels than mainstream females or males. These differences were not significant. The average total scores across year groups were close. There was no consistent trend, up or down, from Year 7 to Year 11, although there is an indication of increased anxiety in Year 11, the year in which students take the national GCSE examination.

The same observation regarding similarities applies to the separate items in the test. For example, 'long division without a calculator' (Item 5) was ranked from 2nd to 4th for all but one of the 10 mainstream groups and the dyslexic groups. This could well be a reflection on the way division is taught and understood. The traditional algorithm does make many demands on several sub-skills, not least of which is memory for basic facts and sequential memory. There is also a significant contribution from the ability to organise work on paper.

One of the demands of mathematics is that answers are produced quickly. Item 13 concerning this issue was ranked highly by all groups, while the dyslexic males ranked it higher than mainstream males in all year groups.

Not surprisingly the 'End of term exam' (Item 20) ranked 1st for all 15 groups. 'Taking a written mathematics test' (Item 3) and 'Waiting to hear your score on a mathematics test' (Item 15) were also consistently ranked as causing high anxiety. It could be that our current test culture makes a significant contribution to mathematics anxiety. There is a test anxiety inventory, the TAICA (Lowe and Lee, 2005), which was used to research the impact of tests on students with (and without) learning disabilities (Whitaker Sena et al., 2007).

'Following your teacher's explanation of a new mathematics topic' (Item 19) did not rank highly, though for dyslexic males in Years 7 to 9 it was ranked two or three places higher than for males in mainstream.

More surprisingly, but then perhaps an indirect comment on our consumer society, as well as the way purchases are processed in shops, the item on 'money when shopping' was ranked as 18th, 19th or 20th for the mainstream groups and for three of the dyslexic year groups. For Years 8 and 9 dyslexic males it ranked at 16th.

Items concerning anticipation, 'Opening a mathematics book' (Item 12) and 'Knowing that the next lesson will be mathematics' (Item 1) ranked towards the bottom of the list for all groups.

When the ranks were averaged and compared for the mainstream groups and for the dyslexic groups, then the differences that stood out were for 'Long multiplication without a calculator' (Item 7) and 'Learning the hard times table facts' (Item 14). The dyslexic students rated both of these items much higher as a source of anxiety. The items on answering questions quickly and long division without a calculator were also rated higher than in the mainstream sample, but since these two items were ranked high out the 20 items by the mainstream sample, the difference was less marked.

'Hearing your score on a mathematics test' (Item 15) was ranked much lower by the dyslexic group than the mainstream pupils, which may be due to the specialist schools managing this issue more sensitively.

Perhaps the relatively low ranking of word problems (Item 4) was unexpected, but the high ranking of long division and fraction questions was not a surprise. It could be that the seemingly irrational procedures taught for these two topics inevitably lead to anxiety. It is interesting to note the much lower ranking of anxiety levels for division when a calculator is available, but experience tells me that this is not necessarily an educational, in the sense of the understanding of mathematics, benefit.

There were relatively few gender differences in ranking.

The results of the survey using the questionnaire highlighted some of the cognitive and affective areas of mathematics that create anxiety for students in secondary schools in England. The levels of anxiety are relatively consistent across ages and gender and dyslexic males, with the same items being ranked similarly in all of the groups.

Examinations and tests created high anxiety levels in all groups. The lower anxiety levels in dyslexic students for tests show that this anxiety can be managed, but the universal top ranking of the end of term mathematics exam (Item 20) for all groups shows that students view this activity negatively.

How to administer the mathematics anxiety questionnaire

A questionnaire for adults is available (free) on my website, www.stevechinn.co.uk

The questionnaire can be used in its entirety or questions can be selected. It can be done independently by the student, before or during the assessment/diagnosis, or in conversation with the student.

How I feel about mathematics: teacher's sheet

The twenty items on this sheet are about mathematics and your feelings when you have to do each one of these things. I would like you to listen to each item and then decide how anxious that situation makes you feel.

If it **never** makes you feel anxious write **1** in the space, if it makes you feel anxious **sometimes** write **2**, if it makes you feel anxious **often** write **3** and if it **always** makes you feel anxious write **4**. So the scores range from 1 for never anxious to 4 for always anxious.

1) Knowing that the next lesson will be a mathematics lesson.

2) Being asked to do mental arithmetic during a mathematics lesson.

3) Having to take a written mathematics test.

4) Doing word problems.

5) Doing long division questions without a calculator.

6) Doing long division questions with a calculator.

7) Doing long multiplication questions without a calculator.

8) Doing fraction questions.

9) Revising for a mathematics test that is going to be given the next day.

10) Doing mathematics homework.

11) Looking at the marks you got for homework.

12) Opening a mathematics book and looking at the set of questions you have to do.

13) Having to work out answers to mathematics questions quickly.

14) Trying to learn the times tables facts.

15) Waiting to hear your score on a mathematics test.

16) Showing your mathematics report to Mum or Dad??

17) Answering questions the teacher asks you in mathematics classes.

18) Working out money when you go shopping.

19) Following your teacher's explanation of a new mathematics topic.

20) Taking an end of term mathematics exam.

How I feel about mathematics: student sheet

Name _____ **Male/Female Date** _____

Year Group_____ **Date of Birth** _____

Does the situation make you anxious?
    1 never   2 sometimes   3 often   4 always

Write your answers here

1) ___ The next lesson.

2) ___ Mental arithmetic.

3) ___ A written mathematics test.

4) ___ Word problems.

5) ___ Long division questions without a calculator.

6) ___ Long division questions with a calculator.

7) ___ Long multiplication questions without a calculator.

8) ___ Fraction questions.

9) ___ Revising for a mathematics test.

10) ___ Mathematics homework.

11) ___ Looking at marks for your homework.

12) ___ Opening a mathematics book.

13) ___ Working out mathematics answers quickly.

14) ___ Learning the hard times tables.

15) ___ Hearing your score on a mathematics test.

16) ___ Showing your mathematics report.

17) ___ Answering questions in mathematics classes.

18) ___ Working out money when shopping.

19) ___ Following your teacher's explanation.

20) ___ Taking an end of term mathematics test.

Statistical data for the test is given in Tables 7.1, 7.2, and 7.3.

Table 7.1 The average total score, the standard deviation for each group and the sample size

Group	7M	7F	7D	8M	8F	8D	9M	9F	9D	10M	10F	10D	11M	11F	11D
Average	37.4	40.6	44.5	37.7	40.0	40.4	36.7	39.7	38.5	35.3	38.6	37.6	36.9	41.5	40.5
SD	10.6	10.2	11.7	12.4	10.8	11.5	11.0	10.6	9.9	10.4	10.6	10.9	11.3	11.4	10.5
Sample size	255	236	59	190	212	88	251	172	119	199	198	107	178	193	69

Total Sample: 2526

Table 7.2 Percentage of students in each group with high anxiety scores (scores >59)

Group	7M	7F	7D	8M	8F	8D	9M	9F	9D	10M	10F	10D	11M	11F	11D
% >59	3.9	4.3	10.1	6.1	6.2	5.7	3.1	3.5	6.7	2.0	3.5	4.7	3.4	5.3	2.9

Table 7.3 The rank order for each item for each group

Item	7M	7F	7D	8M	8F	8D	9M	9F	9D	10M	10F	10D	11M	11F	11D
1	17	17	18	19	17	19	17	17	18	17	18	17	17	18	18
2	14	9	12	14	6	11	10	9	14	16	9	14	12	8	14
3	3	4	5	2	2	5	4	2	4	3	3	3	3	4	6
4	12	16	13	13	13	10	14	10	11	11	14	11	10	12	11
5	2	5	3	3	4	2	3	4	2	4	4	2	4	2	2
6	20	18	20	17	19	20	18	18	20	19	17	18	18	17	17
7	9	11	7	7	10	6	15	11	13	8	11	9	13	10	9
8	8	7	6	12	6	7	8	8	8	7	6	6	8	7	4
9	6	6	3	4	9	4	5	6	4	5	8	5	5	5	6
10	10	13	15	9	14	15	11	16	13	10	13	13	13	16	8
11	16	14	14	16	15	17	9	14	16	14	14	16	16	15	15
12	18	19	17	17	20	18	20	20	19	20	19	20	19	20	20
13	5	2	2	5	5	1	6	5	3	6	7	4	6	6	5
14	11	12	7	10	8	9	16	11	7	13	12	8	15	13	13
15	4	3	9	6	3	8	2	3	6	2	2	6	2	3	3
16	6	8	11	8	11	12	7	7	8	9	10	10	7	9	9
17	15	10	16	15	12	14	12	13	15	12	5	12	9	11	16
18	19	20	19	20	18	16	18	19	16	18	20	19	20	19	19
19	12	15	10	15	16	12	13	15	10	15	16	15	11	14	11
20	1	1	1	1	1	1	1	1	1	1	1	1	1	1	1

8 The 15 minute norm-referenced mathematics test: Basic computations and algebra designed to compare performances

> 'Can you do Addition?' the White Queen asked. 'What's one and one and one and one and one and one and one and one and one and one?'
>
> 'I don't know,' said Alice, 'I lost count.'
>
> The Queen gasped and shut her eyes, 'I can do Addition,' she said, 'if you give me time – but I can't do Subtraction under any circumstances.'
>
> (Lewis Carroll, *Through the Looking Glass*)

One of the frequently asked questions is, even if not phrased so bluntly, 'How serious is the problem?' which means 'How far behind/adrift is this person?' It is probable that the answer will be along the lines, 'About 4 years behind' or 'Working at the level of a 10-year-old' or 'Performing at the first percentile'. All of these are ways of quantifying the magnitude of the problem.

Of course, answers along these lines provide information that may be pertinent to the situation. The answer gives some indication of the severity of the problem, but it is only a summary, there is no information about the causes, roots and manifestations of the problem or indeed any information on appropriate interventions.

The unsophisticated, raw answer to the 'How serious is the problem?' question will come from the use of a standardised norm-referenced test (NRT). So, if that information is required, then a NRT has to be part of the test protocol.

The 15 minute mathematics test provided in this chapter has been normed on a population of over 2500 students and adults from across the UK. Over 50 schools and colleges were involved in providing data.

This 15 minute mathematics test is, like the other components of the battery, optional. Its prime purpose is to assess the level at which the subject is working as compared to his/her peers. It is, by its nature, an overview, a summary.

It can be used with an individual or with a group

There is an obvious inverse relationship between the length of a test and the depth of its content. The 15 minute mathematics test covers a range of arithmetic and algebra tasks, but is primarily a test of arithmetic. There are no questions on geometry, shape and space, or data handling. There are no word problems (see Chapter 12). In fact, vocabulary is kept to a minimum.

Norm-referenced scores can be used to compare to an individual's score to other students' (usually a peer group) scores. However, the 'How did you do that?' question can change normed data into clinical information. Test items may generate errors that can provide some direct diagnostic information for an individual and for the group. This aspect of the test is discussed in detail in Chapter 9.

The 15 minute mathematics test is not dissimilar to the arithmetic test in the WRAT-4 (Wide Range Achievement Test), or the Numerical Operations test in the WIAT-ii (Weschler Individual Achievement Test). However, it was constructed to allow the subject to demonstrate procedural (and conceptual) knowledge by using accessible number facts rather than number facts that may act as a barrier for the person attempting the test. For example, to check 3-digit × 3-digit multiplication, the multiplication facts needed to compute the answer are 2 × and 3 ×. To check the addition of two fractions with different denominators, knowledge of the 2 × and 5 × facts is sufficient.

The language component is minimised so as not to disadvantage those with reading and mathematics vocabulary problems. Of course, symbols have to be used extensively. There is an opportunity to check the subject's knowledge of symbols with other tasks (see Chapter 12).

Some items are included because they can identify common errors (see Chapter 9) and also to elicit other diagnostic information, which might then be followed up in further testing. For example, item 12, 33 – 16 may show the use of a procedural approach, as in:

$$
\begin{array}{r}
^2\cancel{3}\,^1 3 \\
-\ \ 1\ 6 \\
\hline
1\ 7 \\
\end{array}
$$

rather than a more intuitive approach, such as counting on, via 20 and 30. A diagnosis is not just about answers being right and wrong, but about how they were achieved.

The initial versions of the test were trialled and then modified. The final version is the fifth modification.

Even when being exceptionally careful, it is possible for a test designer to make a mistake. For question 17, that is 38.6 – 4, in Version 1 I had presented this as:

$$17.\qquad 38.\ 6-4$$

with an extra space (unintentional) between the '8.' and the '6'. Understandably the question generated the answer '2' several times. The subjects had assumed that this was question 38 and it was asking for 6 – 4. Changing all question numbers to italics and removing the space cured this problem.

A test such as this is likely to cause some negative reaction such as anxiety or stress, so presenting the test at the most appropriate moment in an individual assessment will be important. That moment is not going to be at the start of the assessment. It is best to establish a relationship first and then explain that at some stage you will need to use a short test. Again there will be a balance and a judgment in how this is done. Flagging up the test may reduce stress levels when the test is actually presented to the subject, but it may also generate a stress reaction while you are still working on preliminary items.

(While collecting data from adults, I re-titled the 'Test' as a 'Survey' in an attempt to lower anxiety, decrease negative reactions and encourage more adults to 'have a go' and provide data. The tactic was marginally successful.)

If the test is being used as a screener with a group then this is less of a problem as the circumstances are then quite different. The test can be introduced as a quick exercise in finding out what students know in order to plan/inform future teaching.

In both circumstances you will be trying to minimise debilitating anxiety in order to obtain a performance that best reflects the person's ability and achievement level.

The test items

The test is designed to make retrieval of basic facts less critical to the successful completion of every item. In other words the test is trying to examine procedures rather than a test of recall from memory of basic facts (which is tested in other separate tests, see Chapter 6).

Each item has been chosen to provide diagnostic information as well as contributing to the overall standardised score. Such information may be apparent on looking at the answers, but it is more reliable, when the test is over, to use the follow up question, 'How did you do this?' This can supply confirmation of particular understandings, methods and strategies or may reveal a range of different methods and strategies. Some of these diagnostic aspects are also addressed in other activities in the protocol.

The following explanations are illustrative, not exhaustive. They explain why an item has been chosen for inclusion in the test. You should expect some original, unpredictable answers. Some students will be creative and original in their interpretations of each question (see Chapter 9 on errors).

Item *1.* $2 + 5 =$ _____   answer 7

This addition could be done by counting all, by counting 5 onto 2, by counting 2 onto 5, or by 'just knowing'. Of the three counting strategies, counting 2 onto 5 is the most sophisticated, showing an overview of the question before operating counting mode. An awareness, even if intuitive, of the commutative property of addition shows a good sense of number operations.

Some will multiply instead of adding. This error can occur even with subjects who achieve a high score on the test.

Item *2.* $7 + 8 =$ _____   answer 15

As well as retrieval from memory, this addition could be done by counting all, by counting 8 onto 7 or 7 onto 8, by working via 10 ($7 + 3 + 5$ or $8 + 2 + 5$) or by relating the question to a doubles fact, $7 + 7$ or $8 + 8$ and then adding or subtracting 1 to readjust. Using doubles is another example of a more sophisticated 'linking facts' strategy.

Item *3.* $19 - 4 =$ _____   answer 15

This is the first subtraction item. It could be approached by counting back, which is not an easy skill for many young learners (nor for older ones, too). It will take longer to count on from 4 to 19. The question involves a two-digit number. Can the learner recognise the subtraction is restricted to the units digits and is asking, in effect for $9 - 4$?

Item *4.* $5 + 4 + 3 =$ _____   answer 12

This is a two-step addition. It checks if the learner can add cumulatively. The addition may be adjusted to be $5 + 4 + 1 + 2$ by those who look for 10 facts. As with item 1, even high scoring subjects may make a computational (careless) error here.

Item *5.* $34 = 4 +$ _____   answer 30

This is testing an awareness and understanding of place value and has reversed the 'places', putting the unit first. This makes the item a little more challenging. A number of subjects from the norm-referencing process did not attempt this item. This is the first item that requires the subject to think about/interpret the question.

Item *6.* $400 + 600 =$ _____   answer 1000

This item is testing knowledge of the number bond for 10 taken up to a number bond for 1000. The basic number bond fact is the same, but units have been replaced by hundreds. It checks, in part, if the pattern of $6 + 4$ has been extended to higher place values.

Item *7.* $100 - 58 =$ _____   answer 42

This could be considered as a 'reverse number bonds for 10' item, so $8 + \mathbf{2} = 10$, then $10 + 50 = 60$, finally $60 + \mathbf{40} = 100$, giving an answer of 42.
   It could also be solved in an inchworm/procedural way:

$$
\begin{array}{r}
{\scriptstyle 9\ 1} \\
{\cancel{10}\ 0} \\
-\ 5\ 8 \\
\hline
4\ 2
\end{array}
$$

Item *8.* $16 - 8 =$ _____   answer 8

This is a subtraction version of the double fact ($8 + 8 = 16$). The 'doubles' are facts that seem to be more readily retrieved from memory. The item could be solved by counting back in ones, or in two steps as -6 and -2. It can be solved by counting on, if the subject appreciates the link between addition and subtraction.

Item *9.* $\begin{array}{r} 36 \\ +\ 54 \\ \hline \end{array}$ answer 90

A vertical addition using number bonds for 10 in the units column and requiring 'carrying'.

Item *10.*   827   answer 122

   -705
   $\overline{}$

A vertical subtraction, three-digit from three-digit numbers, with no renaming required, but involving a zero in the tens column. An insecure understanding around zero may create an error in the tens column. Some subjects may perseverate and add the two numbers.

Item *11.* $9 = \_\_ - 4$ answer 13

This item presents a familiar fact in a less familiar form. It can be solved by putting the symbols into words, such as, 'What number minus 4 gives 9?' or 'What number is 9 + 4?' and thus may test if the subject can interpret questions other than literally. It could be related later in an informal post-test 'talk through' to an algebra item such as 9 = y – 4 to explore if the subject can make that link.

Item *12.*   33   answer 17

   $- 16$
   $\overline{}$

This item can be solved by renaming

$$^2\cancel{3}\,^13$$
$$-\ 1\ 6$$
$$\overline{\ \ 1\ 7}$$

which, like item 7, shows a tendency to use procedures. The subject may make an error in the renaming.

   The question can be solved by methods that work more in terms of viewing the numbers involved rather than focusing on a procedure. For example, by comparing 36 – 16 (= 20) to 33 – 16, and adjusting the answer from 20 to 17. It can be solved by counting on from 16, possibly using numbers rather than counting in ones, using 16 + **4** (20) then adding **10** (for 20 + 10 = 30), then adding **3**.

   The common error of 'taking the little from the big' results in an answer of 23.

Item *13.*   Round 551 to the nearest 100   answer 600

Although this works out as a relatively 'easy' item in terms of successful answers, it is included to check a sense of place value and estimating.

Item *14.* Fill in the missing number: 81, 72, __, 54, 45   answer 63

Again, an item that attracts many correct answers, but it does check sequencing skills. There are two sequences occurring concurrently, the tens digit is going down and the units digit is going up.

Item *15.* $60 - 17 = \underline{\hspace{2cm}}$ answer 43

This item involves a zero, so adds to information on how well that concept is understood. The numbers are presented in horizontal format. They may be re-written in vertical form by the procedural subjects. This is usually followed by renaming the 60 as 50 and 10. Some will add on from 17, showing flexibility and inter-linking of the operations. It is another setting for the number bonds for ten.

Item *16.*
$$
\begin{array}{r}
37 \\
42 \\
73 \\
+68 \\
\hline
\end{array}
$$
answer 220

The column addition allows for the use of number bonds for 10 in both the units and the tens columns. Subjects who count as their default adding strategy are more likely to make errors in these sub-additions. The item tests the 'carrying' aspect of place value. An error which shows a lack of understanding of place value is '2020'. Another is '40'. Both these answers reveal a tendency not to review or appraise an answer against an estimate.

Item *17.* $38.6 - 4$ answer 34.6

This is the first item to include a decimal number. The classic error is to ignore or not recognise or not understand the decimal and answer 38.2

Item *18.*
$$
\begin{array}{r}
103 \\
-96 \\
\hline
\end{array}
$$
answer 7

Again this reveals the procedural subject. The item generates renaming errors. Those who are more number oriented can 'see' that the answer is 7. Counting on and thus crossing the 100 is also an effective method. Some errors result in answers, such as 93 or 97 or 107 that again show that answers are not appraised against an estimate.

Item *19.* $2\overline{)38}$ answer 19

This is a traditional short division problem. The data from the norm-referencing process showed that this is an item that many people will avoid. Despite its seemingly simple challenge, it generates errors which suggest that many people have a very poor understanding of division.

If the problem is viewed in terms of the numbers used, it could be seen as being close to $40 \div 2$ and then adjusting the 20 to 19.

In terms of the traditional approach, it will be dealt with something like, 'How many twos in three? One and one left over. How many twos in eighteen? Nine.' This explanation is more procedural than conceptual.

$$2\overline{)3^1\,8} \;\; \begin{array}{c} 1\;9 \\ \hline \end{array}$$

Item *20.* $10\overline{)6030}$ answer 603

This item is often not attempted or an answer of 63 is written. This may be the consequence of an imperfectly remembered procedure, 'Ten divided into 60 is 6, 10 divided into 30 is 3.' The answer 0603 appeared several times, not wrong, but it suggests a literal use of a procedural approach.

   Dividing by 10 and powers of 10 is a fundamental and key skill.

Item *21.* $534 + 185 = 185 + \rule{2cm}{0.4pt}$ answer 534

This item checks knowledge of the commutative property. It can also be done the long way which is to add 534 and 185 and then subtract 185. This approach often results in errors. The item is also about whether a problem is overviewed rather than started impulsively.

Item *22.* $-3 + 13 = \rule{2cm}{0.4pt}$ answer 10

The item presents a subtraction in a different format/sequence to that of early experiences. –3 can be viewed as a 'negative' number.

Item *23.*   Write 'forty thousand and seventy' as a number.   answer 40,070

This item tests how well place value is understood for larger numbers. The most likely errors are 4070 and 4,000,070. Once again it is the concept of zero that challenges basic understanding of mathematics.

Item *24.*   2 ¼ hours = ___ minutes   answer 135

The most common error is '145', where the ¼ hour is interpreted as ¼ × 100 (= 25 and 120 + 25 = 145).
Time introduces base 60 and base 12. As these bases are unfamiliar, they can create errors. If the subject fails on this item then further diagnostic questions can be used later. Time introduces several new concepts as well as new bases, for example, a circular number line, so it is often not well understood. Early misconceptions may re-appear under test conditions.

Item *25.* $\dfrac{1}{4} = \dfrac{}{12}$ answer 3

Another item with 1/4 and thus loosely connected to the time item (24) which also used 1/4. The multiplying number is 3, which should be accessible to the majority of subjects. It is testing the important concept of equivalent fractions.

Item *26.*   1km ÷ 5 = ____ metres   answer 200

This is one of only two items on units of measurement. The dividing number is 5, chosen for its accessibility so that the concept can be tested, not basic fact knowledge. Answers to this item can be bizarre, for example '2010, 1005, 1.5', or suggest place value problems, for example, '0.2 or 20'. This is an item that is often not attempted.

Item *27.*   472   answer 1076
                    526
                  $\underline{+78}$

Addition items are usually attempted. This is no exception. Errors tend to be basic fact errors or place value errors.

Item *28.*   4.8 + 5.21 + 6 = _____   answer 16.01

Mixed decimals and a whole number can cause problems for those who are not secure with the concept of decimal numbers. An estimate would give an answer of about 16. Wrong answers that are a long way from 16 suggest that checking was not done and that a purely procedural approach, without any acknowledgement that decimal numbers are involved, was used.

Item *29.*   20% of 140 = _____   answer 28

There was a low success rate for this item in the data for the norm-referencing of the test, particularly from adults. Again the numbers chosen meant that it was the concept of percentages that was being tested and not the recall of basic facts. The question could be done via a formula

$$\frac{20}{100} \times 140 = 28$$

or by interpreting 10% as 1/10 thus giving an interim answer of 14. 20% is then computed by doubling 14 to give 28.

Item *30.* 2^3 = _____   answer 8

This item tests an understanding of symbols and notation. If the subject does not know the notation then the answer may be given as '6'. '2 × 2 × 2' is not acceptable as a correct answer.

Item *31.* $\frac{4}{7} + \frac{2}{7}$ = _____   answer $\frac{6}{7}$

The classic procedural and conceptual error results in an answer of 6/14 occasionally cancelled down to 3/7 .

This reflects the subject working with symbols rather than words. They are not trying to interpret or make sense of the question. Instead they are using addition as the default operation (like Lewis Carroll's Queen). So, if asked verbally 'What is two sevenths plus four sevenths?' the answer should be 'Six sevenths'. This question (after the test has finished) may reveal the confusion caused by the symbolic representation of fractions. The '6/14' error may be caused by the literal and simplistic interpretation of the + symbol rather than an understanding of the hidden ÷ symbol in written fractions. This issue creates a similar error in Item 38.

Item *32.* $23 \div 1000 =$ _____   answer 0.023

Division by 10, 100, 1000 is a fundamental skill demanding secure understanding of place value, including decimal place value. The role of 0 is again critical. Also the answer, 0.023, is not an everyday mathematics experience. For example, if this were measurement we would use 23 mm.

Some subjects reversed the problem and attempted 23)1000

Item *33.*   541   answer 109,823
                                 × 203

Again, 'easy' multiplying numbers have been chosen so that the procedure can be the focus.

The zero in the tens place in 203 may result in a partial product of '000' or '0000' being written. This would be further evidence in revealing a tendency to make literal interpretations of numbers and procedures.

There was evidence from the norm-referencing data that a grid method (not Napier's bones) had been taught to some subjects, but it rarely resulted in a correct answer. This method seemed to be taking the partial product concept used in 'traditional' long multiplication and changing the emphasis to process rather than understanding.

Success rates on this Item were low. The frequency of no-attempts was high.

Item *34.*   £4.98 + £2.99 + £9.98 = _____   answer £17.95

This is an addition that could be encountered in any shop, where there is a culture of pricing items as .99p or .95p or some other pence value close to £1. It can be done by adding the numbers as they are written, or probably by re-writing them in a column. This is a literal interpretation (Inchworm) which requires good skills with addition. Often there is no pre-calculation estimation, nor any appraisal of the answer.

The addition can also be done by rounding up each price to the whole pound value, then adding £5 + £3 + £10 and subtracting 5p. This is more of a grasshopper method.

Item *35.*   150% of £64 = _____   answer £96

Some people do not realise that there can be percentages over 100 (even though they may have heard soccer managers telling their team to give 'a hundred and ten per cent').

The question can be done via a formula

$$\frac{150}{100} \times 64$$

or as 1×64 plus $\frac{1}{2} \times 64$, probably interpreting 150% as $1\frac{1}{2}$

Item *36.*   Write 0.125 as a fraction _____ (in its simplest form)   answer $\frac{1}{8}$

This is one of only four questions in the test that uses words as instructions. Subjects have to know what 'simplest form' means. Some subjects may make the link that 0.125 is half of 0.25. Others may get as far as '125/1000' and not be able to cancel down.

Item *37.*   5.67 km = _____ metres   answer 5670

This Item requires the subject to know that 1 km is 1000 metres. It also requires an understanding of place value. Instead, many people have a partial recall of mnemonics, such as 'move the decimal point three times for $\times 1000$' or 'add a zero when you multiply by 10'. They are distracted and/or overwhelmed by the .67. The range of errors for this Item was large. Most errors suggest that the rules/mnemonics are not accurately recalled. The most frequent error was 5067 (see Chapter 9).

Item *38.* $\frac{2}{5} + \frac{3}{8} =$ _____   answer $\frac{31}{40}$

This is a more complex fraction question than Item 31. Unlike Item 31, reading the question in words, 'two fifths plus three eighths' does not lead directly to a correct answer. Some answers from the norm-referencing data showed evidence of a procedural approach

$$\frac{2}{5} \times \frac{3}{8}$$

Others used inappropriate addition giving $\frac{5}{13}$

Item *39.* $9\overline{)927}$ answer 103

This Item tests the concept of division combined with a clear grasp of place value. Some answers, for example 13, suggest that there is no appraisal or estimate of the answer.

Item *40*. $6 \div 0.5 =$ _____   answer 12

This Item is a division where the answer is bigger than the number being divided. It challenges a simplistic, restricted view of division as 'making things smaller'. It is also more of a challenge to the person who relies on formulas without interpretation and understanding. If the question is re-worded as, 'How many halves in six?' there is more chance of a correct answer.

Item *41*. $2y + 5 = 31$ $y =$ _____   answer 13

This is a basic algebra question. The norm-referencing data suggests that some subjects found this easier than some of the computation Items, if they attempted it!

Item *42*. $(x + 15) + (x - 23) = 44$ $x =$ _____   answer 26

In the standardising samples, this Item was often not attempted, or the attempts were disorganised. Some treated it as $(x + 15)(x - 23)$. The brackets seemed to trigger quadratic equation mode.

Item *43*. $-13 - (-7) =$ _____   answer –6

To answer this Item correctly, you have to know the rule for dealing with $-(-7)$. It is unlikely that the correct answer will result from a guess.

Item *44*. $60 = 5a$ $a =$ _____   answer 12

The Item is not too challenging if subjects overcome their fear of algebra. It could be considered less difficult to solve than Item 40, though Item 40 does give the symbol for the operation ($\div$). One of the problems with algebra is that it does 'hide' the operation symbols, for example, with a bracket as in $7(x + 3)$. Some subjects may score well on the basic division fact test, but are not able to transfer that knowledge to algebra.

Instructions for administration

Make sure each candidate has a pen or a pencil. All other equipment should be put away.

'This test has a time limit of 15 minutes. You may not have time to attempt all of the questions. Also there are some questions that are based on work that you may not have covered. Try as many as you can.

Do not write anything until you are told. When you have finished the tests, please write your name and age at the top of page 1'

Mathematics test   15 minutes

Name _____ **Male/Female** _____ **Date** _____ **Age** _____(Y)

1. $2 + 5 =$ ____

2. $7 + 8 =$ ____

3. $19 - 4 =$ ____

4. $5 + 4 + 3 =$ ____

5. $34 = 4 +$ ___

6. $400 + 600 =$ ____

7. $100 - 58 =$ ____

8. $16 - 8 =$ ____

9. $\begin{array}{r} 36 \\ +54 \\ \hline \end{array}$

10. $\begin{array}{r} 827 \\ -705 \\ \hline \end{array}$

11. $9 =$ ___ $- 4$

12. $\begin{array}{r} 33 \\ -16 \\ \hline \end{array}$

13.   Round 551 to the nearest 100:_____

14.   Fill in the missing number: 81, 72, _____, 54, 45

15.   60 −17 = _____

16.   37   17.   38.6 − 4 = ____
            42
            73
         +68
          ‾‾‾

18.   103   19.   2)$\overline{38}$
         − 96
          ‾‾‾

---

20.   10)$\overline{6030}$

21.   534 + 185 = 185 + _____

22.   −3 + 13 = _____

23.   Write 'forty thousand and seventy' as a number: _____

24. 2 ¼ hours = _____ minutes

25. $\dfrac{1}{4}$ = $\dfrac{\square}{12}$

26. 1km ÷ 5 = _____ metres

27. 472
    526
    +178
    _____

28. 4.8 + 5.21 + 6 = _____

29. 20% of 140   = _____

30. 2^3 = _____

31. $\dfrac{4}{7} + \dfrac{2}{7}$ = _____

32. 23 ÷ 1000 = _____

33. 541
    ×203
    _____

34. £4.98 + £2.99 + £9.98 = £ _____

35. 150% of £64 = _____

36. Write 0.125 as a fraction _____ (in its simplest form)

---

37. 5.67 km = _____ metres   38. $\frac{2}{5}$ + $\frac{3}{8}$ =

39. 9)927   40. 6 ÷ 0.5 = _____

41. 2y + 5 = 31   y = _____

42. (x + 15) + (x − 23) = 44   x = _____

43. −13 − (−7) = _____

44. 60 = 5a   a = _____

End

ANSWERS

Mathematics test	**15 minutes**

1. $2 + 5 = 7$

2. $7 + 8 = 15$

3. $19 - 4 = 15$

4. $5 + 4 + 3 = 12$

5. $34 = 4 + 30$

6. $400 + 600 = 1000$

7. $100 - 58 = 42$

8. $16 - 8 = 8$

9.
$$\begin{array}{r} 36 \\ +54 \\ \hline 90 \end{array}$$

10.
$$\begin{array}{r} 827 \\ -705 \\ \hline 122 \end{array}$$

11. $9 = 13 - 4$

12.
$$\begin{array}{r} 33 \\ -16 \\ \hline 17 \end{array}$$

13.   Round 551 to the nearest 100   600

14.   Fill in the missing number: 81, 72, 63, 54, 45

15. $60 - 17 = 43$

16.
$$\begin{array}{r} 37 \\ 42 \\ 73 \\ +68 \\ \hline 220 \end{array}$$

17. $38.6 - 4 = 34.6$

18.
$$\begin{array}{r} 103 \\ -\ 96 \\ \hline 7 \end{array}$$

19. $2\overline{)38}$ with 19 above

20. $10\overline{)6030}$ with 603 above

21. $534 + 185 = 185 + 534$

22. $-3 + 13 = 10$

23. Write 'forty thousand and seventy' as a number   40,070

24. 2 ¼ hours = 135 minutes

---

25. $\dfrac{1}{4} = \dfrac{3}{12}$

26.   1 km ÷ 5 = 200 metres

27.   472
        526
      + 78
        1076

28. $4.8 + 5.21 + 6 = 16.01$

29. 20% of 140 = 28

---

30. $2^3 = 8$

31. $\dfrac{4}{7} + \dfrac{2}{7} = \dfrac{6}{7}$

32. $23 \div 1000 = 0.023$

33.   541
       ×203
        109823

34. £4.98 + £2.99 + £9.98 = £ 17.95

35. 150% of £64 = £96

36. Write 0.125 as a fraction $\dfrac{1}{8}$ (in its simplest form)

---

37. 5.67 km = 5067 metres

38. $\dfrac{2}{5} + \dfrac{3}{8} = \dfrac{31}{40}$

      103
39. 9)927

40. $6 \div 0.5 = 12$

---

41. $2y + 5 = 31$ $y = 13$

42. $(x + 15) + (x - 23) = 44$ $x = 26$

43. $-13 - (-7) = -6$

44. $60 = 5a$ $a = 12$

Norm-referenced data and interpreting the scores

The data was collected from over 2500 pupils, students and adults from over 50 schools, colleges, friends and organisations, from across the UK. Of these 1783 were from schools for pupils and students aged from 7 to 15. The remaining 766, for those aged from 16 to 59, were from a range of sources, including colleges, prisons, postal workers and police. A list of the participating bodies involved in collecting data for this test (and/or the basic fact tests) is given in Appendix 3.

The standard deviations, a measure of the spread of the scores, are fairly consistent across the age range 10 to 15. The average scores show a steady increase with age in almost every case. However, there is an interesting dip at age 12, the age that pupils reach in the first year in secondary education. (See also the dip in scores for the basic fact tests.)

It will come as no surprise that an average score is unlikely to be made up of the same correct items for every individual.

Do remember that these 'measurements' are not to be regarded as having the same precision as you would obtain when measuring the diameter of a steel rod with a micrometer. They are for people, and people tend to be a little less consistent and for so many possible reasons. If for no other consideration than this, you need to base any assumptions, and certainly any conclusions, on more than one source of evidence.

The scores for pupils aged 7 years are too low for more detailed data. Those for pupils ages 8 and 9 years old merit more detail. Tables 8.2 and 8.3 relate a percentile to a score. For values in between those given in the tables there will have to be some sensible interpolation.

The data for ages 10 to 15 years are given in Table 8.4 and relate raw score to percentile rank.

As with the data for 8- and 9-year-olds, there may have to be some sensible interpolation for scores that do not appear in the tables.

The 15 minutes maths test is not designed to measure progress at frequent intervals. There are longer, more comprehensive tests that will do that. It is designed to give a quick overview of the level of achievement of an individual in comparison to his peers. It can provide evidence of low achievement either by percentile or by comparing the score achieved with average scores at other ages.[1] It answers the question, 'How big is the problem?'

However, by looking at the errors (Chapter 9) and the questions that are not attempted, a significant amount of diagnostic information can be extracted as well.

---

1 For example: A 14-year-old who scores 22 can be viewed as being at the 23rd percentile for that age group or as attaining the average score for a 10-year-old. A 10-year-old who scores 13 can be viewed as being at the 13th percentile for that age group or as attaining the average score for an 8-year-old.

Statistical (norm-referenced) data for the test is given in tables 8.1 to 8.9.

Table 8.1 Summary table for the 15 minute mathematics test for pupils aged 7 to 15

Age (years)	Average (max 44)	SD	25th percentile	10th percentile	5th percentile
7	7.8	4.0	5	3	2
8	12.6	5.3	9	7	5
9	17.2	6.2	13	10	8
10	23.0	8.5	18	12	9
11	24.2	8.6	18	14	10
12	22.6	8.8	22	15	9
13	27.9	8.8	22	15	12
14	30.2	9.4	24	16	13
15	31.8	8.7	27	17	15

Tables 8.2 More detailed percentile/scores for pupils aged 8 years

Age 8y	
Average	12.6
SD	5.3
Percentile	**Score**
80	17
75	**16**
60	13
40	11
30	9
25	**9**
20	8
10	7
5	5

Table 8.3 More detailed percentile/scores for ages pupils aged 9 years

Age 9y	
Average	17.2
SD	6.2
Percentile	**Score**
80	23
75	**21**
60	19
40	15
30	13
25	**13**
20	12
10	10
5	8

Table 8.4 Score/percentile for ages 10 to 15 years

Score	10y percentile	11y percentile	12y percentile	13y percentile	14y percentile	15y percentile
44					98	98
43			99.5	98	95	96
42			99	95	93	90
41	99.5	99.5	98.5	94.5	88	85
40	99	99	98	92.5	82.5	80.5
39	98	97.5	97.5	88	77.5	75.5
38	97	96	96.5	85.7	73	70
37	94.5	94.5	96	82	68	65
36	92.5	92	93.5	80.5	63	60
35	88.5	89	91.5	79	58.5	55
34	87	86	89.5	77	54	49.5
33	85	82.5	86.5	71.5	50.5	42.5
32	82	78	84	64.5	48	38
31	79.5	74.5	81	58.5	45.5	33.5
30	77.5	70	76.5	51	42.5	30.5
29	75	65.5	73.5	46.5	39	29
28	70	63	69.5	40.5	36.5	26
27	66	56	64.5	40	33.5	25
26	61	52.5	61.5	34.5	31	23.5
25	56	46.5	55.5	30	29.5	20.5
24	51	44	51	27	25.5	18
23	48.5	39	48	26.5	21	17
22	44	36.5	46	24	19.5	16.5
21	39	33	43	20.5	17.5	15.5
20	34.5	30.5	41	17.5	15.5	13.5
19	31.5	27.5	37.5	15.5	14	11
18	27	24.5	32.5	13.5	12.5	10.5
17	22	22	25	12.5	11	9.5
16	20	19	20.5	10.5	9	6.5
15	16.5	15.5	16.5	10	8.5	5
14	16	11	15	8	6	3.5
13	13	8.5	13.5	6.5	5	2.5
12	9.5	8	12	4.5	3.5	2
11	8.5	6.5	8.5	4.5	3	1
10	7.5	5	7.5	2.5	2.5	0.5
9	5.5	4	6.5	2	1.5	
8	4	3.5	4.5	2	0.5	
7	1.5	3	4.5	1		
6	1	2.5	3.5	0.5		
5		1.5	1.5			
4		0.5	0.5			
3						

Table 8.5 Score/percentile for the 16–19-year-old group

Score	Percentile
44	98
43	94.5
42	91
41	84.5
40	82
39	80
38	75
37	69.5
36	65
35	61.5
34	57
33	53.5
32	48
31	44
30	40.5
29	36
28	31
27	28.5
26	26.5
25	24
24	23
23	21.5
22	19
21	17
20	15
19	11
18	10
17	8.5
16	6.5
15	5
14	3
13	2.5
12	2
11	2
10	1.5
9	1
8	0.6
7	0.4
6	

Table 8.6 Percentile/score 20–29-year-old group

Age 20–29y	
Average	29.6
SD	8.2
Percentile	**Score**
80	37
75	**36**
60	32
40	28
30	26
25	**25**
20	24
10	20
5	13

Table 8.7 Percentile/score 30–39-year-old group

Age 30–39y	
Average	32.0
SD	8.7
Percentile	**Score**
80	40
75	**39**
60	36
40	31
30	28
25	**27**
20	25
10	20
5	16

Table 8.8 Percentile/score 40–49-year-old group

Age 40–49y	
Average	33.1
SD	9.1
Percentile	**Score**
80	42
75	**41**
60	38
40	33
30	29
25	**28**
20	26
10	22
5	17

Table 8.9 Percentile/score 50–59-year-old group

Age 50–59y	
Average	34.7
SD	7.7
Percentile	**Score**
80	41
75	**40**
60	38
40	35
30	33
25	**31**
20	29
10	24
5	20

Finally

A full diagnostic procedure may not always be necessary. The test below, showing all that was attempted, gives enough evidence of serious problems with mathematics .... dyscalculia. Note the tally marks at the top of the page, written there by the person attempting the test.

Maths Test.   **15 minutes**   (© 2009 S Chinn)

M/F   Date 19/05/11   Age 30+ y

_____

1. $2 + 5 =$ 7   2. $7 + 8 =$ 21

3. $19 - 4 =$ 17   4. $5 + 4 + 3 =$ 12

_____

5. $34 = 4 +$ 30

6. $400 + 600 =$ 100000   7. $100 - 58 =$ 19

9 Errors and the 15 minute mathematics test: Recognising and understanding common error patterns

Forget your perfect offering
There is a crack, a crack in everything
That's where the light gets in

Leonard Cohen, 'Anthem'

Errors can be informative. They can show what a learner does not understand and sometimes hint at a reason why. If you are able to ask the learner to explain what they did, then the chances of understanding why they did it become much greater than if you are just interpreting from a written answer. That interpretation can aid the way intervention is designed and constructed to maximise learning.

The classic book on errors, *Error Patterns in Computation*, which has reached 10th edition, is now sub-titled, *Using Error Patterns to Help Students Learn* (Ashlock, 2009).

So, it's not just that an answer is wrong. It's why it is wrong. For example:

$$\begin{array}{r} 33 \\ -16 \\ \hline \end{array}$$

This will often generate the answer 23. The error is based on the belief that subtraction involves 'taking the little from the big', so, in the units column, 3 is taken away from 6. There is also a place value issue here, in that the learner may not realise that the 33 can be re-grouped as 20 + 13 and then the single digit number 6 can be subtracted from the two-digit number 13, using a basic fact, restoring the 'little from the big' belief ... for now.

This example illustrates how mathematics develops and how much care has to be taken not to simplify explanations in a way that creates future errors and misconceptions. In this example the next development may be 3 − 6 = −3. Here the big **is** taken away from the little.

Errors and teaching

Teaching should be a diagnostic activity. This will not happen if teachers and tutors mark work only as 'right' or 'wrong'. Of course, it takes time to recognise and acknowledge errors, but many are predictable and demonstrate specific misconceptions or factual errors, or, if a number of children make the same error on a question then it may be that the question is misleading or it may be that the concept has not been taught in sufficient detail.

A classic error occurs with the addition of fractions

$$\frac{1}{11} + \frac{4}{11} = \frac{5}{22}$$

In marking and collating the data for the 15 minute test (Chapter 8), it became apparent that addition is the default operation for many children and adults (and not just with fractions). In this fraction example, addition was applied to both denominator and numerator. There is logic in this error. The symbol '+' means 'add'. It's just that in this case it means 'only add the top numbers'. Some errors have a logic that exposes an imperfect understanding of a procedure, or a confusion created by the inconsistencies of mathematics (see Chapter 8 in *The Trouble with Maths* [Chinn, 2012]).

Many misconceptions and erroneous procedures are generated as students over-generalise during the learning process.

(Ashlock, 2009)

Teachers generate some errors. As an example, in one of the early trial versions of the screener test, I mistyped question 17. I inadvertently added in a space, so that what the person doing the test saw was:

17.   38. 6 – 4.

They, quite understandably, thought I had slipped Q38 in early and that Q38 was 6 – 4, so the answer they wrote was 2. A decimal point looks exactly like the full stop used after the question number ... of course. Closing the space and making all the question numbers italic (in this case *17*) virtually eliminated that error. The design of worksheets can be very influential on success!

Consideration of the subject's error patterns is an important contribution to the information gathered from a diagnosis. Error patterns often indicate the misunderstandings and incorrect procedures used by the subject. Intervention can then be accurately and appropriately targeted.

In Chapter 13 on criterion referenced tests I will write more about setting up questions to be diagnostic.

Classifying errors

Engelhardt (1977) identified eight error types.

1) Basic fact error

Basic fact errors may be just inaccurate recall of the fact in isolation, for example, 8 + 7 = 14, or they may occur within a computation, for example:

$$\begin{array}{r} 28 \\ +37 \\ \hline 64 \end{array}$$

Engelhardt's analysis of 2279 errors led him to conclude that: 'In all quartiles of ability basic fact errors were the most commonly occurring error.'

A basic fact error that occurs within a computation might be described as a 'careless' error, but it could well be a problem with automaticity, that is, while the subject is focusing on process, they lose an accurate retrieval of basic facts. Within the 2500+ scripts that were marked for norm-referencing the 15 minute test, there were occasions where the mistake that took a score from 44/44 to 43/44 was a simple basic fact error.

It is a good technique for students to check all answers where time allows, or even to make this a priority despite time constraints. It is a fact that 'careless' errors are often as costly as any of the other errors.

2) Defective algorithm

Engelhardt describes this as a 'systematic (but erroneous) procedure'. For example:

$$
\begin{array}{r}
541 \\
\times 203 \\
\hline
1003
\end{array}
$$

$35 \div 5 = 1$ $\quad$ $5\overline{)35}$ with 01 above $\quad$ 'How many 5s in 3? None. How many 5s in 5? One.

$28 \div 4 = 2$ $\quad$ $4\overline{)28}$ with 02 above $\quad$ 'How many 4s in 2? None. How many 4s in 8? Two.

A mix of operations was used in the example below:

$$
\begin{array}{r}
47 \\
+32 \\
\hline
129
\end{array}
$$

Engelhardt noted that this was the error type that most dramatically distinguished highly competent performance. Top performers rarely committed this error.

3) Grouping error

These are rooted in misunderstandings of place value, for example,

$$
\begin{array}{r}
37 \\
42 \\
73 \\
+68 \\
\hline
20 \\
20 \\
\hline
40
\end{array}
$$

4) Inappropriate inversion

The most common example is the 'take the little from the big' error (as shown on page 97)

$$\begin{array}{r} 33 \\ -16 \\ \hline 23 \end{array}$$

Or

$$\begin{array}{r} 5 \\ 67 \\ +18 \\ \hline 121 \end{array}$$

where 7 + 8 is 'fifteen' and the interpretation of fifteen is literal in its order, 'fif' 5 and 'teen' 1, which could be perceived a an inversion, 51 for 15.

5) Incorrect operation

This can be a consequence of perseveration. For example, if the first four questions on a worksheet or test are all addition and number five is a subtraction, the subject may persevere with addition. For some children, for whom multiplication facts are a mystery, 6×7 will be answered as 13.

6) Incomplete algorithm (and 'no attempt')

The pupil may miss steps, for example:

$$\frac{2}{5} \times \frac{3}{8} = \frac{15}{16}$$

or he may simply not attempt the question at all. In a study of the errors made by dyslexic students in basic computations, Chinn (1995), the error that was seen dramatically more frequently with the dyslexic students was the 'no attempt'. This error is actually a strategy to avoid making an error.

Mathematics anxiety can be a contributing factor to errors, with children tending not to try questions that they feel they are unable to complete successfully, thus avoiding errors and protecting self-esteem. Noting which questions get the 'no attempt' treatment should be part of analysis and diagnosis of any mathematics work. Also, the 'no attempt' may well affect the time taken to finish attempting a test or worksheet. In collating the data for the 15 minute mathematics test, the 'no attempt' was a very frequently used strategy, even from competent adult performers. It can prevent negative feedback ad protect self-esteem.

7) Identity errors

These errors involve 0 and 1 and confusion of operations, for example, $4 \div 1 = 1$ or $3 \times 0 = 3$. These errors were seen when marking the basic fact tests (see Chapter 6).

8) Zero errors

Zero is a sophisticated concept and is the source of many errors, for example:

$$\begin{array}{r} 13 \\ 9\overline{)927} \end{array} \qquad\qquad \begin{array}{r} 827 \\ -705 \\ \hline 102 \end{array}$$

Engelhardt found that four error types, basic facts, grouping, inappropriate inversion and defective algorithm accounted for almost all the errors committed in his study.

Some favourite errors from the basic fact tests

$2 \times 5 = 25$

$0 \times 3 = 30$

$3 \times 2 = 32$

$1 \times 8 = 81$ all from a 10-year-old pupil who did know that $2 \times 2 = 4$

$4 \div 2 = 42$

$6 \div 3 = 3.6$

$16 \div 4 = 164$

$20 \div 4 = 20.4$ all from another 10-year-old pupil

$2 \div 1 = \dfrac{1}{2}$

$6 \div 3 = \dfrac{3}{6}$

$50 \div 5 = \dfrac{5}{50}$ from a 12-year-old pupil

and from an 11-year-old pupil:

$2 \div 1 = 1r1$

$3 \div 1 = 1r3$

$6 \div 3 = 1r3$

but, as a starting point for intervention, the pupil was correct for $4 \div 2 = 2$

Errors and the 15 minute mathematics test

The norm-referenced 15 minute mathematics test included in this book (Chapter 8) can provide evidence of error patterns, as can almost any written mathematics work.

Many of the items included in the 15 minute test were designed to expose error patterns. Some were designed to avoid some error patterns, for example, item 33 uses basic multiplication facts that should be in most subjects' repertoire, thus reducing the incidence of basic fact errors (and encouraging more subjects to attempt the item). The principle was to add a diagnostic component into an NRT.

Each item in the 15 minute test has been discussed separately below, but interrelated errors and the overall pattern should also be considered when reflecting on an individual subject's strengths and weaknesses. Some of the items in the test were included to interact and confirm patterns.

Criterion-referenced tests (CRTs, see Chapter 13) can be used to provide further evidence of error patterns identified by the 15 minute mathematics test.

Although error patterns are described for each item in the 15 minute mathematics test, experience tells me that some subjects will make errors that have not been included. Sometimes an error will be inexplicable from written evidence and sometimes even if you are in a position to ask the subject to explain.

Note that some errors may occur in every item and are not therefore listed each time in the following analysis. These errors are:

- basic fact errors;
- incorrect operation;
- incomplete algorithm (no attempt); and
- transposals.

All errors are noteworthy, but special attention should also be given to the items that are not attempted. If possible, ask the subject why the item was not tried.

The 15 minute mathematics test was designed to be given to a group or to individuals. In the latter case, the tester should watch the subject at work. This will give more clues as to what and why the errors occur and, when the test is over the tester can ask pertinent exploratory questions

Item 1. $2 + 5$

Generally speaking, this was a warm-up item that most people answered correctly. One error that was found, often with high scoring subjects was 10, which is an incorrect operation (2×5), probably down to an impulsive response.

Item 2. $7 + 8$

Basic facts errors led to 13, 14 or 16. This could be poor retrieval or inaccurate counting on. Using doubles plus or minus 1 may well address these errors. The answer 56 was given by a few subjects.

Item 3. $19 - 5$

The basic fact error was usually 16. The incorrect operation, probably due to perseveration was 23.

Item 4. $5 + 4 + 2$

Few errors were made with this item. Most were probably caused by inaccurate counting, resulting in 13 or 11. There were 209 out of 225 (93 per cent) correct answers for 8-year-old pupils for this item.

Item 5. $34 = 4 + \_\_\_$

The most frequent error was 38. Eleven $(3 + 4 + 4)$ was given and one 10-year-old pupil changed the symbols of the question making it: $34 + 4 = 37$.
Out of 220 nine-year-old pupils 160 (73 per cent) gave the correct answer.

Item 6. $600 + 100$

Errors included 100,000, 900, 10,000. Primarily the errors were about misconceptions of place value. There were 181 correct answers out of 200 for 11-year-old pupils.
    A 15-year-old student who scored 39/44 answered 1,00,000 for this item. It seems that high scores do not necessarily eliminate all fundamental errors.

Item 7. $100 - 58$

52 was a 'popular' error, which could be attributed to poor retrieval of number bonds for 100 (and due perhaps to not extending knowledge of the number bonds for 10). 58 is a zero error. 158 is the incorrect operation, addition, error. Less explicable errors included 142 and 44. Out of 220 nine-year-old pupils 157 (71 per cent) obtained a correct answer. Out of 108 30-year-old participants 108 (92.6 per cent) obtained a correct answer.

Item 8. $16 - 8$

This is a recall of a doubles addition fact, translated to a subtraction fact. Correct answers were obtained by 78 out 109 (71.5 per cent) seven-year-old pupils, 189 out of 200 (94.5 per cent) 11-year-old pupils and 217 out of 220 (98.6 per cent) 15-year-old students. Errors were close to the correct answer, for example 7 or 9, and usually suggested counting errors.
    Inappropriate inversion triggered by re-writing the question in vertical form produced an answer of '12' from an 11-year-old pupil.

$$\begin{array}{r} 16 \\ -8 \\ \hline 12 \end{array}$$

Item 9.   36
                $+54$

80 was a frequent error, which may be explained by the ten from the units column not being 'carried'. The method by which an erroneous answer of 81 was obtained was apparent from the script:

$$
\begin{array}{r}
\text{t u} \\
36 \\
+54 \\
\hline
81 \\
0
\end{array}
$$

Errors that were likely to be created by basic fact or counting errors included 89 and 91. I was unable to guess the methods that led to 700 and 1860.

For nine-year-old pupils there were 183 out of 220 (83 per cent) correct answers.

Item 10. $\begin{array}{r} 827 \\ -705 \\ \hline \end{array}$

Most of the errors were attributable to the numbers being added rather than subtracted. However, a subtraction led to 102, which is a zero error and 222, a mix of a zero and a basic fact/counting errors.

1532 is a combined incorrect operation and grouping errors as is 15,212.

I think the answer '37' was obtained by adding 8 + 7 and 7 + 5 and 20.

The inclusion of a zero increases the error rate in questions. For 11-year-old pupils there were 149 correct answers out of 220 (68 per cent). For 14-year-old students there were 189 correct answers out of 225 (84 per cent).

Item 11. $9 = \underline{} - 4$

The most frequent answer was 5, which suggests confusing the operation. A 40-year-old who scored 40/44 answered 12 illustrating the occurrence of basic fact errors across all levels of achievement. There was a nine-year-old pupil who wrote on his paper that this was an 'impossible trick'. Other errors included 6, 10 and 15 (which may be a basic fact/counting error). Out of 220 10-year-old pupils 159 (73 per cent) answered this item correctly.

Item 12. $\begin{array}{r} 33 \\ -16 \\ \hline \end{array}$

The most frequent (and predictable) error was 23, resulting from 'taking the little from the big' in the units column, an inappropriate inversion. This was a frequently occurring error for 11-years-old pupils, but quite infrequent for 15-year-old students. The answer 13 was obtained as shown below:

$$
\begin{array}{r}
{}^{2}3\,{}^{1}3 \\
-1\,6 \\
\hline
1\,3
\end{array}
$$

This error used renaming, but still used the inappropriate inversion error. 49 is obtained by adding, an incorrect operation.

There were 111 correct answers from 173 scripts (64 per cent) for 12-year-old pupils and 180 from 220 (82 per cent) for 15-year-old students.

Item 13.   Round 551 to the nearest 100

The most frequent wrong answer was 500, although 550 and, quite rarely 400, was also given. There were 137 correct answers from 225 scripts from eight-year-old pupils and 209 from 225 scripts for 14-year-old students.

Item 14.   Fill in the missing number: 81, 72, ___, 54, 45

The two errors that occurred most frequently were due to pupils focusing on one sequence, either the units (83) or the tens (64). Out of 220 scripts 174 (79 per cent) showed correct answers for nine-year-old pupils. For 13-year-olds the percentage correct was 91.

Item 15.   60 − 17

The answers 57 and 53 were common, probably caused by regrouping errors. 42 was probably a basic fact error and 57 a zero error. Out of 225 scripts for eight-year-old pupils 112 (50 per cent) had correct answers and that improved to 172 out of 220 (78 per cent) for 10-year-old pupils.

Item 16.   37
                42
                73
              +68
              ____

There were many different answers offered for this item. Some were created by place value confusions and some by basic fact errors, for example, 230. Some answers were clearly incorrect, for example, 40 or 2020, but they were written down anyway. The procedure for obtaining 40 was shown by a 10-year-old pupil:

                46
                38
                74
              +62
              ____
                20
                20
                40

I assume that 2020 was obtained by a variation of this.

A high scoring (41/44) 40-year-old answered 221 giving further credence to Engelhardt's observation that basic fact errors occur in all quartiles of achievement.

Of eight-year-old pupils 26 per cent obtained the correct answer, 76 per cent of 10-year-olds were successful.

Item 17.   38.6 – 4

The most frequent error was 38.2, where the place value of the decimal 38.6 was not acknowledged. Despite my correction of the trial version I still had a handful of students who answered 2. Of scripts from 12-year-old pupils 56 per cent had correct answers. This rose to 78 per cent for 14-year-old students.

Item 18.   103
             -96

The combination of a subtraction problem and regrouping across a zero created a range of errors. 193 was a frequently occurring error, a combination of inappropriate inversion and a zero error (0 – 9 = 9). 93 has the same roots, but different outcome. 13 involves an inappropriate inversion in the units column. 197 and 97 involve grouping plus zero errors, for example:

$$
\begin{array}{r}
1 \\
0\overset{\frown}{1}03 \\
-96 \\
\hline
097
\end{array}
$$

The error below, from a 17-year-old student who scored 28/44 shows the triumph of procedure over commonsense, a regrouping error.

18. $\begin{array}{r} {}^{9}1{}^{L} \\ 1\,1\,\bcancel{0}3 \\ -\,96 \\ \hline 1\,07 \end{array}$

Of answers from 11-year-old pupils 68 per cent were correct and 70 per cent from 13-year-old students.

Item 19. $2\overline{)38}$

This is the first item to attract a significant number of 'no attempts', in all age groups, for example, 24 per cent for 11-year-old pupils. Of those attempting it 54 per cent of 11-year-old pupils gave a correct answer. That rose to 61 per cent for 15-year-old students, and 40-year-old adults achieved 85 per cent correct answers. Errors were mostly basic fact based, for example, 16 and 17.

$$
\begin{array}{r}
1\;6 \\
2\overline{)3^{1}\,8}
\end{array}
$$

14 is due to a defective algorithm. 110 is 'unreasonable' and probably an example of a defective algorithm.

Item 20. $10\overline{)6030}$

There were a significant number of 'no attempts' for this item, too, for example, 24.5 per cent of 11-year-old pupils. The most frequent error was 63 (60 ÷ 10 = 6 and 30 ÷ 10 = 3). Correct answers were often written as 0603 and one student showed an inchworm approach:

$$0603$$
$$10\overline{)6^603^30}$$

The percentage of correct answers for 10-year-old pupils was 45 per cent and for 13-year-olds was 49 per cent.

Item 21. 534 + 185 = 185 + _____

This item is about the commutative property of addition. No calculation is necessary. The answer is 534. A significant number of subjects of all ages added 534 and 185 and then subtracted 185 from the total, often making a basic fact error and thus obtaining an incorrect answer. A 40-year-old subject did this procedure accurately, noticed what the answer was and wrote, 'Silly me!'. Fifty-six per cent of answers were correct for 11-year-old pupils and 77 per cent were correct for 14-year-old students.

Item 22. −3 + 10 = _____

The common error is 16. For 10-year-old pupils the percentage of correct answers was 56 per cent. This rose to 84 per cent for 15-year-old students. The question presents a basic fact in an unfamiliar order. Inconsistencies often create confusion.

Item 23. Write 'forty thousand and seventy' as a number.

4070 was the most frequently occurring error. There were many other offers, including 400070, 40,7000, 40700, 4007, 40017, 470, 40,0007 and 1407. All these errors are about place value and the sequencing of digits.

A girl aged 15, who scored 42/44, gave as her answer, *forty thousand and seventy*

Of the 10-year-olds 56 per cent obtained a correct answer and 62 per cent of 13-year-old students were correct.

Item 24. 2¼ hours = _____ minutes

The frequent error was 145 minutes. This takes ¼ hour to be ¼ × 100 = 25 minutes, rather than ¼ × 60 minutes. Other errors included 150, 125 and 175 minutes. Of the 11-year-old participants 58 per cent were correct and 68 per cent of 14-year-old students were correct.

Item 25. $\dfrac{1}{4} = \dfrac{\square}{12}$

This item received a high percentage of correct answers. There was no dominant error. Incorrect answers included 1, 2, 4, 8 and 9.

Item 26.   1km ÷ 5 = _____metres

This item received a significant number of 'no answers' and a range of incorrect answers that suggested that students do not know how many metres are in a kilometre or they unable to divide by 5 or both. Incorrect answers included 500, 1005, 10, 500, 20 and 250. The percentage of correct answers for 12-year-old pupils was 17 per cent and for 15-year-old students 56 per cent. For adults in their 20s it was 51 per cent.

Item 27.
$$\begin{array}{r} 472 \\ 526 \\ +78 \\ \hline \end{array}$$

The errors for this item were largely basic fact errors, resulting in answers such as, 976, 1176, 1074 and 964. All these examples are close to the correct answer. The percentage of correct answers for 11-year-old pupils was 73 per cent and for adults in their 30s it was 90 per cent.

Item 28.   4.8 + 5.21 + 6 = _____

This mixed decimal and whole number item created errors focused on place values, for example:

$$\begin{array}{r} 5.21 \\ 4.\ 8 \\ 6 \\ \hline 9.35 \end{array} \qquad \begin{array}{r} 4.8 \\ 5.21 \\ 6 \\ \hline 10.61 \end{array} \qquad \begin{array}{r} 4.08 \\ 5.21 \\ 6 \\ \hline 15.29 \end{array}$$

There were 85 correct answers out of 200 scripts for 11-year-old pupils (42.5 per cent) and 116 correct answers from 225 scripts for 14-year-old students (52 per cent).

Item 29.   20% of 140 = ____

This is one of two percentage items included in the test. It can be answered by working out 10 per cent and doubling that answer (2 × 14) or by using a formula, $\frac{20}{100} \times 140$ or by using $\frac{1}{5}$

The numbers were chosen to minimise basic fact errors.

Common errors were 7 and 35. 7 was obtained by halving 14 instead of doubling it. 35 from interpreting 20% as ¼. The answer '20' is about reflecting back the question. There were a significant number of 'no attempts' for this item. For 12-year-old pupils the percentage of correct answers was 32. This rose to 58 per cent for 14-year-old students.

Item 30. $2^3 = $ ___

This question is about mathematics code, understanding how we write indices and what they mean. Ignorance of this code leads to the frequent error of 6. A less frequent error, but seen on several scripts was 12. Most likely cause, as evidenced by one student was:

$$2^3 \times 2 \qquad\qquad\qquad 6 \times 2 = 12$$

The scripts for 11-year-old pupils showed 28 per cent correct answers, for 13-year-old students, 49 per cent and for 15-year-old students it was 76 per cent.

Item 31. $\dfrac{4}{7} + \dfrac{2}{7} = $ ___

It will not be a surprise to learn that the (very) frequent error is $\dfrac{6}{14}$ which is sometimes cancelled to $\dfrac{3}{7}$ thus another example of an unrealistic answer and adherence to procedures.

Of 11-year-old pupils 31 per cent were correct and 63 per cent of 14-year-old students gave correct answers.

Item 32. $23 \div 1000$

A significant number of students divided, or attempted to divide 1000 by 23. Errors created by attempting the question by dividing 23 by 1000 included 0.000023 from a 36-year-old who scored 43/44. A 15-year-old student who also scored 43/44 got as far as 23/1000. The decimal point ended up in a very varied number of places. All these errors demonstrated partly remembered rules based around 'move the decimal point' and 'put in some zeros' rather than an understanding of place value with decimals. There were a significant number of 'no attempts', for example, 39 per cent of 13-year-old students did not attempt this question.

A selection of errors from 15-year-old students includes:

0023.00   0.0023   002.3   2.3   000.23   0.23   230   0.00023   0.000023

Of 15-year-old students 47 per cent gave a correct answer.

Item 33.   541
            ×203

This item generated a lot of 'no attempts', even from relatively confident subjects. Even for 15-year-old students, the age for taking the national GCSE in England, 18 per cent were 'no attempts'. While not an error, the inclusion of the line of zeros does indicate a rigid adherence to procedures:

$$
\begin{array}{r}
541 \\
\times 203 \\
\hline
1623 \\
00000 \\
108200 \\
\hline
109823
\end{array}
$$

The grid method seems to be making an appearance, but it does demand good 'organisation on paper' skills before the student gets to any mathematics. The first example below was from an 11-year-old pupil who scored above average at 26/44. The second example below was for a 47-year-old teacher with great organisational skills ... but who still including the line of (unnecessary) zeros.

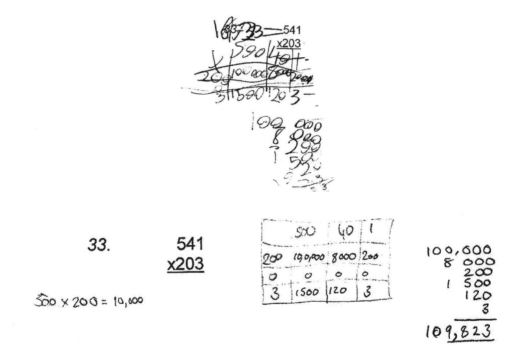

Two common errors were 1003 and 1043. 1003 is obtained by multiplying the numbers in the place value columns, $1 \times 3 = 3$, $4 \times 0 = 0$ and $5 \times 2 = 10$. 1043 is a variation where $4 \times 0 = 4$, a basic fact error to add to the defective algorithm. A less logical variation gives an answer of 10,123, where the procedure is $1 \times 3 = 3$, $4 \times 3 = 12$ and $5 \times 2 = 10$.

There are variations on the place value error for the 2:

$$
\begin{array}{r}
541 \\
\times 203 \\
\hline
1623 \\
000 \\
1082 \\
\hline
2605 \\
1
\end{array}
$$

000   This has the row of zeros. The carried 1 is not added in

$$
\begin{array}{r}
541 \\
\times 203 \\
\hline
1623 \\
10820 \\
\hline
12443
\end{array}
$$

And there is the incorrect operation error:

$$
\begin{array}{r}
541 \\
\times 203 \\
\hline
744
\end{array}
$$

A very successful professional man in his 50s simply wrote, 'too hard'. The 'no attempt' strategy stretches across all ages. Of 13-year-old students 39 per cent did not attempt this question and only 15 per cent answered it correctly, while 14 per cent of 12-year-old pupils and 38 per cent of 15-year-old students answered correctly.

Item 34.   £4.98 + £2.99 + £9.98 = £ _____

This is a 'real life' example. It can be done by an inchworm method of procedural, step-by-step addition or by a grasshopper method of rounding the prices up to whole pounds, adding to make £18.00 and then subtracting 5p. Most of the errors are basic fact errors. Success rates were much higher than for item 33, with 38 per cent of 12-year-old pupils and 55 per cent of 13-year-old students obtaining correct answers, but then it is an addition problem.

Item 35.   150 per cent of £64 = _____

Of 14-year-old students, 33 per cent used the 'no attempt' strategy, 58 per cent achieved a correct answer, which leaves 9 per cent who made other errors. Several of these seem to use 50 per cent, obtaining 32, but also 0.32 and 320. The item is also looking at the concept of a percentage that is more than 100 per cent.

Item 36.   Write 0.125 as a fraction _____ (in its simplest form)

Success rates for 13-year-old, 14-year-old and 15-year-old students were, respectively, 17, 31 and 32 per cent. Errors seem to focus on using 5 or on 4, leading to 1/5, 5/4 and ¼. Errors which showed a lack of understanding of the conversion process included, 1/25, 0/125, 1/125 and 125 per cent. 125/1000 showed an understanding of the conversion principle, but not of 'simplest' form.

A place value confusion gave $\dfrac{125}{100} = \dfrac{5}{4}$ for a 27-year-old who scored 43/44.

Item 37.   5.67 km = _____ metres

This item revealed many errors for multiplying a decimal number by 1000. Most were partial, inaccurate memories of what to do, for example, 'move the decimal point' or 'add zero(s)'. The most frequent error was 5067.

Other errors included:

50.67 (14y)   50,067 (20y)   5.670 (50y)   56.7 (50y)

567 (40y)   05.67 (40y)   500.67 (40y)   5.68 (11y)
567000 (16y)   50670 (15y)   5.68 (11y)

Correct answers were provided by 44 per cent of 14-year-old students and 52 per cent of 40-year-old adults.

Item 38. $\dfrac{2}{5} + \dfrac{3}{8} =$

The most frequent, and predictable, answer was $\dfrac{5}{13}$

Far less frequent is 18, computed by adding all four numbers. A basic fact error (8 × 5 = 35) gave 31/35 instead of 31/40 and a combination multiplying the top numbers (numerators) and adding the bottom numbers (denominators) gave 6/13, interpreted as a defective algorithm.

Partially and inaccurately remembered procedures (or 'defective algorithms') produced some interesting answers:

$$\frac{2 \times 5}{5 \times 8} + \frac{3 \times 8}{8 \times 5} = \frac{10}{40} + \frac{24}{40} = \frac{34}{40}$$

$$\frac{2}{5} + \frac{3}{8} = \frac{1}{3}$$
(with +1 over the numerators and +3 under the denominators)

$$\frac{2}{5} \times \frac{3}{8} = \frac{15}{16}$$

And …. a correct renaming, followed by the most frequent error of adding both top and bottom numbers:

$$\frac{16}{40} + \frac{15}{40} = \frac{31}{80}$$

Only 37 per cent of answers from 15-year-old students were correct. That fell to 21 per cent for 13-year-old students and 28 per cent of 15-year-old students took the 'no attempt' strategy. Generally speaking, if a question is about addition, more students will attempt the question.

Item 39. $9\overline{)927}$

The most frequent error is 13, a place value/grouping error. A more bizarre and very unreasonable answer was 0.009. Only 27 per cent of 11-year-old pupils and 45 per cent of 15-year-old students answered correctly.

Item 40.　　$6 \div 0.5 =$ _____

The most frequent error is 3. Much less frequent errors are 0.3 and 0.12.

Item 41.　　$2y + 5 = 31$　　$y =$ _____

A 17-year-old student who scored 38/44 wrote next to this question 'bad memories' and did not attempt it (and didn't attempt Item 42 either). Some young pupils persevered through to the end of the test, mostly by omitting most of the later items. An eight-year-old who persevered and reached question 41 answered:

$$2y + 5 = 31 \quad y = \text{yards}$$

Some errors are about bringing a current level of (inappropriate) knowledge to a question that is beyond your experience. (That could almost be an observation for life!) A frequent error was '6', also a consequence of inadequate knowledge of the conventions of algebra.

$$2y + 5 = 31$$

$$26 \ + 5 = 31$$

18 resulted from taking +5 across the equals sign (31 + 5). 36 suggests that there was no division by 2 (both examples of 'defective algorithms'), and basic fact errors, for example, $26 \div 2 = 12$ and $31 - 5 = 16$ were again present. The percentage of correct answers for 14-year-old students and 40-year-old adults were close at 59 per cent and 56 per cent, respectively.

Item 42.　　$(x + 15) + (x - 25) = 44$　$x =$ _____

A 35-year-old primary teacher, who successfully answered every other question correctly, wrote, 'Can't do algebra!!' in large writing next to this item. Intervention in mathematics is not always about the numbers and concepts. Addressing attributional style (see Chapter 7 in *The Trouble with Maths* [Chinn, 2012]) is often a key part of any intervention. Perhaps it is the pervasive attitude to algebra, but this question was not attempted by a significant percentage of students. Some treated the question as a quadratic equation and applied a partly remembered mnemonic:

42.　　$(x + 15) + (x - 23) = 44$　　　$x =$ _____

$$x^2 - 23x + 15x - 8 = 44 \ (+8)$$

$$x^2 - 8x - 8$$

Others took a rather convoluted path to their correct answer:

42. $(x + 15) + (x - 23) = 44$ $x = \underline{26}$

$$x+15 = 44 - (x - 23)$$
$$x = 44 - (x - 23) - 15$$
$$x + x - 23$$
$$2x - 23 = 44 - 15$$
$$2x = 29 + 23$$
$$= 52 / 2 =$$

Of 15-year-old students 46 per cent did not attempt this question and 24 per cent gave correct answers.

Item 43. $-13 - (-7) =$ _____

In order to succeed with this question you have to know the rule about 'minus minus'. Errors that were a consequence of not knowing were 20 and –20. These were the most frequently occurring errors. Basic fact errors were sometimes combined with this error to give answers such as 21 and 8. Of 14-year-old students 38 per cent gave correct answers and 37 per cent of 40-year-old adults also gave correct answers.

Item 44. $60 = 5a$ $a =$ _____

The percentage of correct answers among those who attempted this was high. It could almost be seen as an example that algebra is not always as difficult as its reputation suggests. A predictable error was 6. Basic fact errors included 11. One high scoring (37/44) 15-year-old student used a logical sequence to obtain a correct answer:

$$10 - 2$$
$$20 - 4$$
$$30 - 6$$
$$40 - 8$$
$$50 - 10$$
$$60 - 12$$

Summary

It will not be possible to interpret every error from written evidence only. It is tempting to conclude that 'bizarre' errors show serious misunderstandings. Basic fact errors, which could be described as 'careless' errors for high achievers, still cost marks in examinations (and elsewhere). Some errors give useful diagnostic evidence about which concepts are understood or which pre-requisite skills are missing. Trying to understand why errors occur is about trying to understand learners.

The approach to errors and error analysis in some ways illustrates the approach advocated for assessment and diagnosis in this book. It is impossible to cover every eventuality. You have to develop the skills to be observant, innovative and adaptable.

Finally

Proof from a 14-year-old student that two wrongs make a right.

$$
\begin{array}{r}
3\,\cancel{4}\,0^{1}1 \\
-\ 3\,9\,2 \\
\hline
0\,0\,9
\end{array}
$$

10 Thinking (cognitive) style: How learners think through maths problems[1]

If a child or an adult is failing in mathematics, then using intervention that is based solely on practising the same mathematics with the same procedures that have already failed them, continuing to teach them in just the same old way, that intervention is not likely to be successful. The intervention has to be cognisant of the way the learner learns. This chapter is about how learners think and the approaches they use for solving problems. It includes a diagnostic assessment of thinking (or cognitive) style.

Thinking style is closely linked to meta-cognition, which is about knowing, being aware of, how you think, 'knowing about how you know'.

A major project from the National Research Council of the USA published as *How People Learn* (Bransford et al., 2000) identified just three key findings that help people to learn. Finding number three is:

> The teaching of meta-cognitive skills should be integrated into the curriculum in a variety of subject areas.

The Test of Cognitive Style in Mathematics (Bath et al., 1986), around which this chapter is based, was first published in the USA. It was designed to investigate the way that people solved mathematics problems. Cognitive style can be influenced by many factors, for example, long-term memory for facts and procedures, working memory, skills at generalising and conceptual ability. Thus it is another example of the interrelationships of the learning factors covered in this book. The 'test–retest' validity was checked with samples from the USA and from England.

Riding and Rayner (1998) defined thinking (cognitive) style as: 'A person's preferred and habitual approach to organising and representing information.' As a teacher, I have to hope that the word 'habitual' can be challenged. It is my belief that a flexible approach to any problem in mathematics is preferable. Again, there is research to support that belief.

The Bath, Chinn and Knox work described two thinking styles at the extreme ends of a spectrum, the 'Inchworm' and the 'Grasshopper'. The thinking style spectrum is present in children and in adults. Individuals may modify their thinking style as life's experiences take over from school experiences.

---

1 (See also *The Trouble with Maths* [Chinn, 2012: ch. 4].)

The characteristics of the 'Inchworm' – the formula, sequential thinker

On first seeing the problem or task the Inchworm:

- focuses on the parts and details – separates;
- looks for a relevant formula or procedure – they are formula oriented;
- they have a constrained focus, wanting one method.

When actually solving the problem, the Inchworm:

- works in serially ordered steps – forward;
- uses numbers exactly as given;
- is more comfortable with paper and pen – Inchworms document their methods.

Having finished working on the problem, the Inchworm:

- is unlikely to check or evaluate answers;
- if a check is done, then it will be done by using the same method again and thereby repeating any error that was made the first time;
- may not understand the method or procedure used – they work mechanically.

The characteristics of the Grasshopper – the relational, holistic thinker

On first seeing the problem or task the Grasshopper:

- overviews, puts together, is holistic;
- looks at the numbers and the facts to restrict down or estimate an answer – this is not guesswork, it is controlled exploration.

When actually solving the problem, the Grasshopper:

- has a range of methods which are selected according to the problem;
- often works back from a trial answer;
- adjusts, breaks down and builds up numbers, finding the easy numbers and easy number combinations (for example, 5 is treated as half of 10, 98 is 'seen' as 2 less than 100);
- has a good understanding of numbers and their interrelationships and of the operations and their interrelationships;
- performs calculations mentally and rarely documents – Grasshoppers are answer oriented.

Having finished working on the problem, the Grasshopper:

- is likely to appraise and evaluate the answer;
- checks by a different method.

There are a number of interactions with other factors and also some implications for learning and teaching. For example, Inchworms need good long-term mathematical memories and good working memories in order to be successful in mathematics. Grasshoppers need to learn how to document their methods (multiple choice questions remove this requirement).

Perhaps, it might be useful if teachers and tutors took the test in this chapter and discovered their own thinking style. In fact the stimulus for the investigations by Bath et al. (1986) was the observation of their own teaching styles and how well individual students responded to those teaching styles. Thinking style will influence teaching style and a severe mismatch between students' and teacher/tutor's thinking style can have significant impact on learning.

The ever-swinging pendulum of teaching philosophies is illustrated in the two teaching styles, Behaviouristic and Constructivist, as described by Parmar and Cawley (1997). These two styles seem to tally with the Inchworm and Grasshopper cognitive styles. This suggests that students and teachers need to be aware of both styles and thus to teach to both styles.

Behaviouristic

- Focus on developing skills
- Identification of a single algorithm
- Teacher provides sequence of steps
- Students memorise and follow set procedure
- Mastery of skills prior to their application
- Individualised drill and rehearsal activities for mastery

Constructivist

- Focus on deeper level of understanding
- Evolvement of a variety of materials and activities
- Teacher encourages discussions
- Students interact with materials to develop conceptual learning
- Students assimilate new concepts into prior knowledge

The Behaviourist style will favour the Inchworm learner and the Constructivist will favour the Grasshopper learner. In an ideal world, both thinking styles and both teaching styles will be used in a balanced and appropriate way. This could even be an argument against those pendulum swings that seem to introduce so many trends and philosophies in education. Learners need cognitive flexibility to access both styles.

The cognitive (thinking) style test

As with all the tests in this book, it is designed to be 'user-friendly'. So,

For those tested:

1 The test is short, around 20 minutes, but often less.
2 The test items have been selected to minimise test anxiety.
3 There is no time constraint.
4 The test is focused on the methods used to obtain a solution rather than on a correct answer.
5 The final analysis is concerned with thinking style. It does not make judgments about ability.
6 The test is administered individually and is designed to encourage discussion.

For the assessor/tester:

1 The test is short, taking around 20 minutes.
2 The items have been selected to minimise anxiety.
3 The test is quick and easy to score.
4 The 'Cognitive/Thinking Style Profile' is quick to construct and interpret.
5 The results can be discussed openly with the subject as the emphasis is not focused on correct answers and is not, therefore, judgmental.
6 Any test that is administered individually gives more information.
7 It is not necessary to use every item in every case. Assessors can make their own judgment about what is appropriate for an individual.

Interpreting the test results

The following explanations are a guide. The individuality of people makes it impossible to list and describe all the variations that will be experienced when using the test. The most frequently met answers are discussed and the way they are interpreted should be a guide for interpreting any other method.

Item 1A. (Mental arithmetic)   230 + 98   answer   328

Inchworm

The problem is visualised as 230 in the traditional written vertical form and then
$$+98$$

solved sequentially, working from right to left, adding the units, 0 + 8, adding the tens, 3 + 9 and 'carrying' the 1 from the 12, adding 1 and 2 giving a final answer of 328.

This method requires a good working memory. It generates the answer as 8 (units), then 2 (tens) then 3 (hundreds), a sequence that has to be reversed to 328.

Variations which involve adjusting the 98, for example adding 70 and then adding 28 or adding 90 and then 8, but do not change 98 to another number, are mid-way Grasshopper strategies and should be scored as 1 along the Grasshopper scale.

Grasshopper

The 98 is adjusted to 100 and added to the 230 to make 330. The 330 is then adjusted by subtracting 2 (98 = 100 − 2) to give 328.

I showed a 34-year-old art graduate this problem. She explained that she could use the 'round up to 100' method for 99 and 98, but 97 was too challenging in the requirement to count back 3.

The same interpretations apply to Item 1B. 48 + 99.
This modification can be used for younger or less confident subjects.

Item 2A.   (Mental arithmetic)   230 − 97   answer   133

Inchworm

The problem is visualised as 230

−97

The subtraction is performed sequentially from right to left as though it were written on paper.

For the units, the task is 0 − 7. Assuming the zero errors of 0 −7 is 0 or 0 − 7 is 7 are not done, the subject has to rename the 30 by moving to the tens column:

$$2\ 10$$
$$2\ \cancel{3}\ 0$$

The subtraction in the units column is now 10 − 7 = 3.
The next step is to move to the tens column, where the task is 2 − 9. This also requires renaming, using the hundreds digit

$$1\ 12$$
$$\cancel{2}\ 2\ 0$$

The subtraction is now 12 − 9 = 3 and the final answer is 133.
This is a longer procedure than the addition and makes heavier demands on working memory for the Inchworm thinker. The evidence from the data collected to provide the norm-referenced data for the 15 minute mathematics test in this book showed that subtraction is a weaker skill than addition.

Grasshopper

The 97 is taken up to 100 by adding 3. The subtraction is 230 − 100 = 130. This is a smaller answer than the accurate answer. 3 is added back to give 133.

The Grasshopper thinker is able to round up to a number that makes the subtraction easier and appreciate and understand the relationship between the 97 and the 100 and the consequences of using the rounded number. Learners with a Grasshopper thinking style interrelate numbers and are then able to adjust the interim answer, again using an ability to interrelate numbers and to appreciate that subtracting 100 instead of

97 results in a 'low' interim answer and thus requires a compensatory addition (of 3 in this example). This requires a good sense of number.

The same interpretations apply to Item 2B. 136 – 99.
This modification can be used for younger or less confident subjects.

Item 3   (Mental arithmetic)   2 × 4 × 3 × 5   answer 120

Inchworm

The learner using an Inchworm thinking style starts at the beginning number (2), possibly encouraged by 2 × facts being accessible from memory, and multiplies sequentially:

$$2 \times 4 = 8 \quad 8 \times 3 = 24 \quad 24 \times 5 = 120$$

Some Inchworm thinkers may be unable to calculate the last step, 24 × 5.
This question is often a good example to show that the subject is not predisposed to overview a question before starting, neither for estimation purposes nor for selecting an efficient procedure.

Grasshopper

The learner using a grasshopper thinking style overviews the problem and adjusts the order of multiplication, using key facts and numbers (in this example, 2, 5 and 10)
    2 × 5 = 10 and 4 × 3 = 12 (which might be done as 3 × 2 × 2) then 10 × 12 = 120
This item provides further evidence of the literal approach of the Inchworm and the adapting/adaptable approach of the Grasshopper.

Item 4   (Mental arithmetic)   95 ÷ 5   answer   19

Inchworm

The learner using an Inchworm thinking style uses a short division procedure.
    9 ÷ 5 = 1   remainder 4

    45 ÷ 5 = 9 final answer 45

possibly visualising the problem as it would be written on paper $5\overline{)9^4 5}$ with 19 above

Grasshopper

The learner using a grasshopper thinking style 'sees' the 95 as close to 100 and divides 100 by 5 (or knows and uses a multiplication fact 20 × 5 = 100). The 20 is then adjusted down to 19. This is using a conceptual approach, often working with multiplication rather than division, probably using 'lots of' instead of the abstract word 'multiply', even if this is done subliminally. The method shows an understanding of division as it links to multiplication and uses estimation or the link of 9 to 10.

Interpreting the results for the four mental arithmetic items only

Mental arithmetic activities require a number of pre-requisite skills.

The mental arithmetic questions require the Inchworms to have a good working memory and a good retrieval memory (or efficient strategies) for basic facts. Inchworms use numbers literally, for example, 9 is not 'seen' as 1 less than 10. Questions are not overviewed or interpreted. Thus an Inchworm thinking style for these mental arithmetic questions requires a good working memory for dealing with long, multi-step proc-esses and a good long term memory for basic facts and for procedures.

The Grasshopper thinking style needs a good sense of numbers and operations and their interrelationships to be successful. The methods used make less demand on working memory. Key facts are used whenever possible. The numbers are adjusted so that most of the calculation is done using key numbers. Questions are overviewed, interpreted, computed and the answer is adjusted when necessary.

Thinking style can be very influential on success levels in mental arithmetic and consequently on much of the mathematics people meet in everyday life, such as checking a bill for a meal out, first by an estimate and then more precisely if the estimate gives cause for concern.

Thinking style will link to performance in the basic fact tests. These facts can be considered to be basic mental arithmetic tasks (using linking strategies) rather than solely as an exercise in rote memory. The ultimate Inchworm thinker strategy for addition is to finger count. (Note that any use of counting points towards Inchworm thinking.) The Grasshopper thinking style will involve relating numbers, so that 9 + 5 may be computed via 10 + 5 = 15 then take away 1 from 15 to obtain 14, or 7 + 8 may be computed as 8 + 8 − 1. Pupils with an Inchworm thinking style are less likely to develop linking strategies without guidance, instruction and practice. The instruction is likely to need visual images or materials/manipulatives or both.

Back to the test …

Item 5 (Written arithmetic) Addition of a column of numbers

```
   8
   6
   3
   4
   7
   2
 + 6    answer   36
```

Inchworm

The learner with an Inchworm thinking style will add the numbers in the sequence in which they are presented, top to bottom or bottom to top. They will not overview the numbers. They are unlikely to make a pre-computation estimate.

Grasshopper

The learner using a Grasshopper style will overview the numbers and note any combinations that make ten, for example, 8 and 2. They will pair all tens. This gives three pairs and a 6 left over, so a total of 36. They may make a pre-computation estimate based on the question having 7 numbers and then multiplying 7 by an estimated average value (an estimate within an estimate). May be they will choose an estimated average value of 5, so $7 \times 5 = 35$. This may also be done to check the answer. (See also Item 16 in the 15 minute mathematics test.)

Item 6.   (Written arithmetic)   600   *answer 102*
$$-498$$

Inchworm

The learner with an Inchworm thinking style will use renaming/regrouping procedures, or possibly 'borrow and pay back'.

```
     9
  5 10 0            6  0  0
  6  0 0            5  9 10
 -4  9 8           -4  9  8
 ───────           ────────
  1  0 2            1  0  2
```

(the intermediate line strategy)

Grasshopper

The learner with a Grasshopper thinking style will probably not document any part of the process, only writing the answer 102, which is obtained by rounding 498 to 500, subtracting 500 from 600 and adding back 2. The evaluation question for the intermediate (100) answer is, 'Is the answer bigger or smaller?' This question may be difficult for an Inchworm thinker. Students using a Grasshopper thinking style are more likely to use this question, successfully and/or subliminally, than an Inchworm thinker.

Item 7.   (A word problem)   Red pens cost 17p. Blue pens cost 13p. If I buy two red pens and two blue pens, how much do I pay?   Answer   60p

> Notes: If necessary, the question can be read to the subject
>   For younger children, the prices may be changed to 7p and 3p

Inchworm

The learner with an Inchworm thinking style interprets the question literally and calculates in three steps:

$$2 \times 17 = 34 \qquad 2 \times 13 = 26 \qquad 34 + 26 = 60p$$

Grasshopper

The learner with a Grasshopper thinking style notes that 17 and 13 add to make 30 (using key facts, the number bonds for 10) and multiplies 30 by 2 to get 60p, thus calculating the cost of two times (red pen + blue pen)

Item 8.   (A word problem, but primarily a sequence problem)

If these are the first 14 letters, what is the 23rd letter in this sequence?
abcdeabcdeabcd ....
Answer c

Inchworm

The learner with an Inchworm thinking style will use a counting strategy, for example, counting along the dots from 15 to 23, then reciting the letters to match the numbers until the 23rd letter, c, is reached. There is less influence from working memory if this is solved using a written record of the steps.

Grasshopper

The learner with a Grasshopper thinking style will see a pattern, 'abcde', which repeats four times for 20 letters, thus making the 23rd letter c.
    If the learner cannot process information in chunks of 5, then this Grasshopper strategy will not be appropriate. Thinking style can be influenced by several factors.

Item 9.   (A word problem involving time)   A film starts at 7.40 pm and ends 1 hour 50 minutes later. At what time does the film finish?   Answer   9.30 pm

A younger learner or anyone who found the first version hard could try an easier version of the question, modified so that the film ends 50 minutes later.

Inchworm

The learner with an Inchworm thinking style will add the hour and then the minutes (or vice-versa), so 7 + 1 = 8pm 40 + 50 = 90 minutes = 1 hour 30 minutes

$$8 \text{ pm plus } 1 \text{ hour } 30 \text{ minutes} = 9.30 \text{ pm}$$

or the 50 minutes will be split, using 20 minutes to take the 7.40 to 8.00. Then the 1 hour is added to take the time to 9.00 and then remaining 30 minutes takes the time to 9.30 pm.

Grasshopper

The learner with a Grasshopper thinking style will round the 1 hour 50 minutes to 2 hours, then add 2 hours to 7.40 to get 9.40. The added 10 minutes have to be subtracted, giving 9.30 pm. The 50 minutes is seen as close to one hour. This link is known and used.

This is one of only two items on time in the tests included in the protocol. Further investigation should be done by following up on the evidence the items provide, probably by using clinical questions.

The next three items look at shapes.

Item 10.   There are 49 squares in the figure below. How many are black?

   Answer   49

Inchworm

The learner with an inchworm thinking style will:

Count the black squares, or

Count rows, $4 + 3 + 4 + 3 + 4 + 3 + 4$ or

Count the black squares down one side and across one side and multiply $4 \times 4 = 16$, forgetting, or not seeing, the three rows of 3 black squares and obtaining an answer that is not reasonable.

The Inchworm thinker sees the details in the figure.

Grasshopper

The learner with a Grasshopper thinking style will see that there are almost the same number of black and white squares. They, intuitively, know that there are more black squares, so the split is 25 black (24 white). They may note that the corners are black or that the middle square is black to obtain the evidence for 'more black'.

The Grasshopper thinker is using a holistic approach, seeing the whole picture first.

Item 11.   There are 25 squares in the figure below. How many have a cross?

X	X	X	X	X
X				X
				X
X				X
X	X	X	X	X

Answer 15

Inchworm

The learner with an Inchworm thinking style will:

Count the crosses, or

Count the three sides as having 5 crosses each, over-counting the corner squares, to get 15, plus the extra 2, making 17. Sometimes the 'quicker' strategies that Inchworm thinkers use are not successful.

Grasshopper

The learner with a Grasshopper thinking style sees the pattern of $3 \times 3 = 9$ blank squares in the middle, adds the extra one from the left hand side to get 10, which is subtracted from 25 to give 15.

Item 12.   What is the area of the 'horse'? How many little squares in the 'horse'?

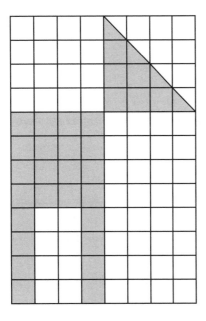

Inchworm

The learner with an Inchworm thinking style will:

Perceive the 'horse' as a triangle, the 'head', a square, the 'body' and two lines/ rectangles, the 'legs'. They may use the formula for the area of a triangle, that is, $\frac{1}{2} \times$ base $\times$ height, $\frac{1}{2} \times 4 \times 4 = 8$. Then they will add $4 \times 4 = 16$ for the area of the 'body' and 2×4 for the 'legs', giving a total of 32.

An extreme Inchworm style is to count all the squares, using the half squares in pairs to make one square.

Grasshopper

The learner with a Grasshopper thinking style will recognise that the triangle is half of a 4×4 square and that the gap between the 'legs' is also half of a 4×4 square. Moving the triangle into the gap creates two 4×4 squares (or one 8×4 rectangle) and thus an area of 32.

Note that the three shape and space items may reveal a different cognitive style to the numerical items.

The test of cognitive style in mathematics (TCSM)

The test can be photocopied and presented to the subject on A5 cards or paper, one item at a time. Observation and Answer sheets are provided for photocopying after the questions.

After each item ask, 'Can you explain to me how you did that?' and (sometimes) 'Can you think of another way of doing the question?'

Item 1A. (Mental arithmetic)

$$230 + 98$$

Item 1B. (Mental arithmetic)

$$48 + 99$$

Item 2A. (Mental arithmetic)

$$230 - 97$$

Item 2B. (Mental arithmetic)

$$136 - 99$$

Item 3. (Mental arithmetic)

$$2 \times 4 \times 3 \times 5$$

Item 4. (Mental arithmetic)

$$95 \div 5$$

Item 5. (Written arithmetic)

```
    8
    6
    3
    4
    7
    2
  + 6
  ___
```

Item 6. (Written arithmetic)

```
   600
  −498
  ____
```

Item 7.

Red pens cost 17p. Blue pens cost 13p. If I buy two red pens and two blue pens, how much do I pay?

Item 8.

If these are the first 14 letters, what is the 23rd letter in this sequence?
abcdeabcdeabcd ....

Item 9A.

A film starts at 7.40 pm and ends 1 hour 50 minutes later. At what time does the film finish?

Item 9B.

A film starts at 7.40 pm and ends 50 minutes later. At what time does the film finish?

Item 10.

There are 49 squares in the figure below. How many are black?

Item 11.

There are 25 squares in the figure below. How many have a cross?

X	X	X	X	X
X				X
				X
X				X
X	X	X	X	X

Item 12.

What is the area of the 'horse'? How many little squares in the 'horse'?

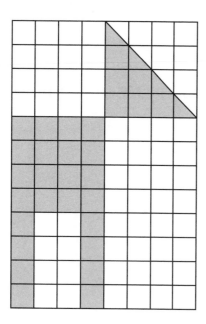

TCSM Observation Sheet

Name _____ Date _____

1A.   230 + 98

1B.   48 + 99

2A.   230 − 97

2B.   136 − 99

3. $2 \times 4 \times 3 \times 5$

4. $95 \div 5$

5.
```
   8
   6
   3
   4
   7
   2
  +6
```

6.   600
     −498

7.   Red pens cost 17p. Blue pens cost 13p. If I buy two red pens and two blue pens, how much do I pay?

8.   If these are the first 14 letters, what is the 23rd letter in this sequence?
                     abcdeabcdeabcd ....

9A.   A film starts at 7.40 pm and ends 1 hour 50 minutes later. At what time does the film finish?

9B.   A film starts at 7.40 pm and ends 50 minutes later. At what time does the film finish?

10.   There are 49 squares in the figure. How many are black?

11.   There are 25 squares in the figure. How many have a cross?

12.   What is the area of the 'horse'? How many little squares in the 'horse'?

TCSM Work Sheet

Name _____ Date _____

1A.   230 + 98 = _____

1B.   48 + 99 = _____

2A.   230 − 97 = _____

2B.   136 − 99 = _____

3.   2 × 4 × 3 × 5 = _____

4.   95 ÷ 5 = _____

5.
```
    8
    6
    3
    4
    7
    2
  +6
  ___
```

6.
```
   600
  −498
  ____
```

7.   Red pens cost 17p. Blue pens cost 13p. If I buy two red pens and two blue pens, how much do I pay?

8.   If these are the first 14 letters, what is the 23rd letter in this sequence?
     abcdeabcdeabcd ....

9A.   A film starts at 7.40 pm and ends 1 hour 50 minutes later. At what time does the film finish?

9B.   A film starts at 7.40 pm and ends 50 minutes later. At what time does the film finish?

10.   There are 49 squares in the figure. How many are black?

11.   There are 25 squares in the figure. How many have a cross?

12.   What is the area of the 'horse'? How many little squares in the 'horse'?

The TCSM Profile Line

Name _____ **Date** _____

The Profile Line can be completed to give a visual representation of cognitive style.
Each Inchworm answer 'scores' 2 on the left hand side of the central zero.
Each Grasshopper answer 'scores' 2 on the right hand side of the central zero.

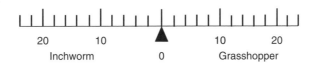

A separate line could be used for the three shape and space items, 10, 11 and 12

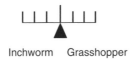

11 Estimation: A key maths life skill to help develop more confidence with maths

Estimation is a life skill. There are many occasions when an estimate will suffice, for example, a tip in a restaurant, buying timber for DIY jobs, cooking, working out how long a journey will take. Estimation requires a different attitude to precise computations and a different way of thinking (see Chapter 10). Estimation requires a sense of number and value and an appreciation of the place values of key numbers such as thousands, hundreds and tens, for example, 933 could be estimated to the nearest hundred, 900 or the nearest thousand, 1000.

Estimation can also make use of the 'Is it bigger or smaller?' question. An estimate of 933 to 900 is an estimate that is smaller than the true value. An estimate of 1000 for 933 is an estimate that is bigger than the true value. The question, 'Is it bigger or smaller?' is also about sense of number.

Estimation also requires the skill of appraising how far 'off' the estimate can be to work, to be appropriate, in the circumstances in which it is being applied. Being able to estimate is a sophisticated skill, involving number sense, place value and the appropriate use of number values in a range of contexts.

A key underlying concept is, as it often is, place value. For example, estimating 933 to 1000 takes a three-digit number to four digits, it takes a hundreds number to thousands. (Examples such as this could be viewed as rounding as well as estimating.)

Estimation takes you (usually) to 'easier' numbers and so calculations using the estimated numbers should also be easier. It can also be about taking 'difficult' numbers and operations and re-interpreting them to make 'easy' numbers, for example, dividing by 2 instead of multiplying by 0.5. There is a need to develop flexibility in how numbers are interpreted and modified. The person who 'sees' numbers literally, for example, seeing 9 as simply 9 and not as 1 less than 10, an Inchworm characteristic, will find estimation a difficult challenge. This characteristic may also handicap the development of number sense, sense of magnitude and comparison of magnitudes.

Grasshoppers tend to be good at estimating; Inchworms tend not to be.

It is, perhaps, not surprising that one of the observations from the National (US) Mathematics Advisory Panel (2008) was that poor estimation performance often reveals underlying difficulties in understanding mathematics in general. And the Missouri Longitudinal Study of Mathematical Development and Disability found that number line accuracy became more important across grades in maths (Geary, 2010).

Dyscalculia and subitising

Two pre-requisite skills are included in the Dyscalculia Screener (Butterworth, 2003). One of them is 'subitising', the ability to know how many dots appear, randomly arranged, on a computer screen. The number of dots presented ranges from two to nine. I have worked with many students who do not have this skill, even with small numbers, for example, a 14-year-old pupil who did not know, without counting 'How many fingers?' when I held up three fingers. It may be possible to address this problem by using a variety of exercises based on estimation.

Coins and dots tasks

Two tasks on estimation are included in the informal tests that can be used as part of a diagnostic session (see Chapter 4). One is to ask for an estimate for a relatively large number, about 35, of 1p coins spread out on a table. The other is the estimation of a number of dots on a card, first linearly and then randomly arranged. This time, a smaller quantity, around 12 dots, is used.

These tasks make a low stress start to a diagnosis. Estimates are not definitively wrong. Unlike basic fact questions, for example, if the answer '14' is given for 'What is 7 plus 8?' it is wrong. If the question was 'What is an approximate answer, an estimate, for 7 plus 8?' then '14' is not wrong. It is best to avoid generating too many failures in the early stages of a diagnostic procedure. Failures tend not to motivate.

Empty number lines

```
0                              100
```

```
0                              0.1
```

Empty number lines can be used to explore estimation skills. The lines could be 0 to 10, 0 to 100, 0 to 1000 or beyond, or could be decimal number lines such as 0 to 0.1 and 0.01 to 0.1 or even a 0 to 1 number line for estimating fraction values, all used as appropriate for the subject.

The task of being able to place, say 7 on a 0 to 10 line is about estimating, but could also be about the ability to proportion the line as 7:3 (and thus, via tenths to 7/10 and 3/10).

Estimation requires a good sense of number (values) and an understanding of the interrelationships between numbers and the four operations.

The number line tasks can be flexible and adjusted to the responses from the subject. They can be used directly as in 'Place a mark where you think 70 would be on this 0 to 100 number line' or with some guidance as in asking this via an intermediate step, for example, asking the subject to place 50 and then to place 70.

I used a metre rule to explore this ability in a 14-year-old boy. He marked his estimate on the (blank) back of the rule and then I turned it over to compare this with the gradations. The rule made the task more practical and realistic for him. His success rate was impressive and gave him a positive feeling about maths for the first time for many years. Of course, the outcome may not have been that successful, but one of the encouraging characteristics of estimation tasks is that the answers are not definitively wrong, just 'close' or 'not so close'. Often in a diagnosis one is seeking strengths and positives on which to build intervention, rather than focusing only on the weaknesses and negatives.

Number lines can also be used to remind learners that the start of the number line is 0 and not 1.

Estimation and checking an answer

One of the lasting impressions I will have of marking the 2500 (an estimate!) tests I used for setting up the norm-referenced 15 minute test (Chapter 8) is of too many 'wild' answers, answers that were a long way from any reasonable estimate, to questions, for example:

```
    37
    42
    73
  +68
  ───
    40
```

(from a 17-year-old student who scored 39/44)

```
   541
  ×203
  ────
   2030   (it was lined up like this)
```

(from an 11-year -old student who scored 25/44, 1 mark above average for that age group)

Mathematicians make mistakes. What distinguishes a successful mathematician from one who fails is that they usually notice and check their mistakes. Maybe it is that the mathematics' culture of doing maths quickly contributes to the avoidance of checking answers. Maybe it is an Inchworm characteristic, that is, doing a maths problem once is enough, checking it as well is a step too far. Maybe it is a lack of flexibility (or a fatalistic attitude) interpreted as, 'If I did it wrong this way the first time, I'll probably only do the same the next time.'

The question, 'Can you give me an approximate idea of what the answer might be, an estimated answer?' could be used for both the examples above after the test has been finished and, indeed, for any arithmetic question from the test.

Using estimating for checking is a key mathematics skill for life.

Being unaware of an estimated value for a computation is one of the dangers of over-reliance on calculators.

In the Bryant et al. (2000) study of what teachers in the USA considered to be characteristic behaviours of students who have teacher-identified maths weaknesses, number 9 on a list of 33 characteristics was 'Reaches "unreasonable" answers.' Ranked 4th was 'Fails to verify answers and settles for first answer.'

Estimating and the test protocol

There is not a separate, stand-alone test for estimation in this book. May be there will be a standardised, norm-referenced test in a later edition. One reason for this 'omission' is that the skill of estimation can be explored within the tests and exercises already available in this book.

- The informal, introductory procedure (Chapter 4) includes two exercises on estimation.
- A metre rule that is blank on the reverse side can be used as a number line.
- Several of the items in the Thinking Style test (Chapter 10) lend themselves to supplementary questions, such as 'Can you give me an estimate, a guess at an approximate answer for this problem?'
- The 'Can you give me an estimate ...?' question can be used at different places and times within the protocol to give information from a number of settings.

Thus there are several opportunities of investigate the skill of estimation, enough to provide adequate evidence of ability or difficulty.

12 Mathematics vocabulary and word problems: Exploring how they contribute to maths learning difficulties

In an ideal world, word problems would be used to challenge the learner's understanding of mathematics. They would be a valuable and valid addition to the curriculum. Instead they have a reputation for confusing learners and for a lack of reality in their content.

> Students come to know that they are entering a realm in which common-sense and real world knowledge are not needed. Students learn to ignore contexts and work only with the numbers.
>
> *(Boaler, 2009: 46–47)*

Word problems do create difficulties for many children, particularly those with mathematics weaknesses. In their study of the characteristic behaviours of such children, Bryant et al.'s (2000) the top three characteristics (out of 33) were:

- Has difficulty with word problems.
- Has difficulty with multi-step problems.
- Has difficulty with the language of mathematics.

However, word problems are part of the curriculum and so children and adults need to learn how to solve them. The test in this chapter is a criterion-referenced test (CRT) and is included, as are all the tests, to be used if appropriate. It is also included as an exemplar that can be adapted to construct similar tests for group and individual diagnostic purposes.

One of the best strategies for teaching children how to understand word problems is to encourage them to create their own from a number sentence, a 'reverse translation' (Sharma, 1985). One of the most effective approaches to learning how to solve word problems is the Singapore Model Method (Kho Tek et al., 2009).

Before any examination of the cognitive issues there should be a check for the obvious (Chapter 4). The questions, 'Can they see?' 'Is the paper/print contrast an issue?' 'Can they read the question?' 'Do they understand the key words?' 'Can they read the non-technical (names, objects, etc.) words?' 'Are they slow readers?' 'How successful is their reading comprehension?' may reveal crucial information.

Symbol/vocabulary matching cards

> 'It is largely by the use of symbols that we achieve voluntary control over our thoughts.'
>
> *(Skemp, 1986: 78)*

Two sets of cards are given at the end of this chapter. They can be used before the word problem sheet is given to check familiarity with the range of mathematics vocabulary that is used for the four operations. This matching activity is usually low stress, so could be used as a 'break' from more demanding tasks used in an assessment/ diagnosis. Any gaps in mathematics vocabulary should be recorded, particularly in terms of the vocabulary used in any follow-up word problem sheet. You need to be sure that you are testing what you think you are testing.

The word problem sheet in this chapter was constructed on the assumption that the subject has a full knowledge of the range of mathematics vocabulary used. It is a clinical decision as to whether or not these words should be explained as the subject attempts the questions. The sheet spans quite a broad range of question styles, starting with a very basic construction and ending, only seven questions later, with a quite complex structure. You may well decide to focus on a narrower breadth in the sheets that you design, using more examples for each criterion. (For more background on vocabulary and word problems see *The Trouble with Maths* [Chinn, 2012: ch. 6].)

Example of a structured word problem test sheet

If the test is used with an individual, careful observation and questioning will provide more information on how the questions are solved. The questions focus on the four operations. The structure of each question is explained below.

It may be necessary to read the questions to the subject.

1. What is 8 subtract 5?
   The digits are in the same order as they will be for the number sentence 8 – 5. 'Subtract' is a technical word (as opposed to 'take away'). 'Minus' could be substituted for 'subtract'.
   This is a single digit minus single digit subtraction.

2. Take away 3 from 9.
   The digits are now in reverse order for the number sentence required to solve the problem, that is, 9 – 3. The computation is still single digit.

3. What is 48 more than 42?
   This is a question that is similar to Item 9 on the 15 minute mathematics test. It may reveal a difference in ability for the two tasks.
   (It may be worth comparing other word problems against equivalent/similar number only problems.)

4. Sam had 28 CDs left after he gave 3 to Mike. How many CDs did Sam have before?
   'Left' and 'gave' usually infer subtraction. Not so here. If the strategy is to circle the numbers and the key word, then this will be treated as a subtraction. Does the subject read the question for interpretation or is the approach impulsive?

5. Jay deletes some photos from his camera and has 34 left. He takes 6 more photos and then deletes 15 more. How many photos does he have now?

This is a two-step question using two 'subtraction' words, 'delete' and 'left'. 'More' which normally infers addition is used once for that purpose and then again in a phrase that infers subtraction. Does the subject try to model or draw a picture for the problem before solving it? What strategy is used?

6. Kev has £50. Mike has £20. Kev spends £32. How much money does Kev have left?

   The information about Mike is superfluous. This can create difficulty for insecure or impetuous learners. Careful observation could give an indication as to how or whether the problem is overviewed before the subject begins to try and solve it.

7. Zak charges £8 to clean a car. He cleans six cars in the morning and four cars in the afternoon. How much does Zak earn that day?

   This is a three-step question, two multiplications and one addition or a two-step question, one addition and one multiplication. This item lends itself to the question, 'Can you think of another way of solving this problem?' And can be used to discuss:

   $8 \times 6 = 48$ $8 \times 4 = 32$ $48 + 32 = 80$

   $8 \times 6 + 8 \times 4$

   and

   $8 \times (6 + 4)$

8. Olly is buying a new car. The cost of the car is £9000. He puts down a deposit of £1800 and has to pay the balance in 20 equal monthly payments. How much is each monthly payment?

   This is a two-step question, first subtraction, then division. There are no key words for the operations, but the structure of the question is logical. The word 'each' might hint at division.

Word problems

Name _____ **DoB** _____ **M/F** _____ **Date** _____

1. What is 8 subtract 5?

2. Take 3 from 9.

3. What is 48 more than 42?

4. Sam had 28 CDs left after he gave 3 to Mike. How many CDs did Sam have before?

5. Jay deletes some photos from his camera and has 34 left. He takes 6 more photos and then deletes 15 more. How many photos does he have now?

6. Kev has £50. Mike has £20. Kev spends £32. How much money does Kev have left?

7. Zak charges £8 to clean a car. He cleans six cars in the morning and four cars in the afternoon. How much does Zak earn that day?

8. Olly is buying a new car. The cost of the car is £9000. He puts down a deposit of £1800 and has to pay the balance in 20 equal monthly payments. How much is each monthly payment?

Word problems Observation Sheet

Name _____ **Date** _____

1. What is 8 subtract 5?

2. Take 3 from 9.

3. What is 48 more than 42?

4. Sam had 28 CDs left after he gave 3 to Mike. How many CDs did Sam have before?

5. Jay deletes some photos from his camera and has 34 left. He takes 6 more photos and then deletes 15 more. How many photos does he have now?

6. Kev has £50. Mike has £20. Kev spends £32. How much money does Kev have left?

7. Zak charges £8 to clean a car. He cleans six cars in the morning and four cars in the afternoon. How much does Zak earn that day?

8. Olly is buying a new car. The cost of the car is £9000. He puts down a deposit of £1800 and has to pay the balance in 20 equal monthly payments. How much is each monthly payment?

Basic information Observation Sheet

Name _____ **Date** _____

Can they see?

Is the paper/print contrast an issue?

Can they read the questions? (Reading age: Test............... RA...... Date.........)

Can they read the non-technical words?' (names, objects, etc.)

What is their level of reading comprehension? (Test .... Date ....)

Are they slow readers/writers?

Do they understand the key mathematics vocabulary?

Word and symbol cards

Photocopy and cut out the cards on p. 145 or write the symbols and words on blank playing cards. Place the five symbol cards as column headings and ask the subject to place the correct words into the appropriate columns. Note the responses on the Observation Sheet.

Observation Sheet. Matching Words and Symbols.

Name _____ **Date** _____

$+$

$-$

$\times$

$\div$

$=$

Note correct and incorrect matches. The question, 'Can you find another place where this word might fit better?' could be used for any incorrect matches.

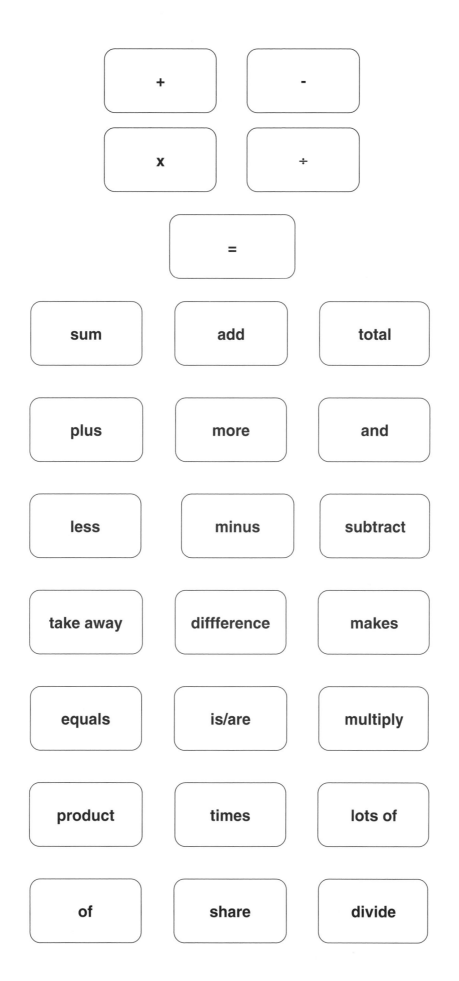

| + | - |
| x | ÷ |

| = |

sum	add	total
plus	more	and
less	minus	subtract
take away	diffference	makes
equals	is/are	multiply
product	times	lots of
of	share	divide

13 Criterion-referenced (formative) tests: Focusing on identified problems and showing how to build ongoing diagnosis into teaching

> Criterion-referenced testing can reach its full potential only when it is so integrated into the day-by-day functioning of the classroom that it cannot be easily separated out as a testing activity.
>
> *(Hofmeister, 1975: 78)*

Criterion-referenced tests (CRTs) measure a person's level of proficiency in performing a set of skills or in mastering set objectives. They measure what a student can and cannot do in an absolute or personal sense, that is, not in comparison with other students.

CRTs focus in on specific objectives, skills and tasks. They provide far more detailed information than norm-referenced tests (NRTs), but, consequentially take up much more time.

They can be used for evaluating teaching and interventions by using them as pre- and post-tests. They can be used to follow up diagnostic clues from other tests such as NRTs and to provide further on-going diagnostic information by showing which criteria are mastered and which need further intervention. An analysis of the errors the students make can reveal further diagnostic information (see Chapter 9) and thus inform the content of CRTs. CRTs can be used to provide information for setting up IEPs (individual education plans) and to identify the objectives that can take a student to a desired goal.

Virtually any worksheet or homework sheet can be set up to measure criteria and to identify errors and misconceptions (see Chapter 9). Not every question needs to be criterion-referenced, but inclusion of some will make worksheets far more informative. This can make diagnosis an on-going activity, integrated into the teaching programme as Hofmeister suggests. Setting up a sound resource base of such worksheets and homework sheets could be a cooperative activity for all the teachers of mathematics in a school or college.

Criteria

Ashlock et al. (1983) lists 24 criteria for whole number subtraction. If a test were constructed to cover whole number subtraction, even if one item were given for each criterion when constructing a test or worksheet, the result would be a very long test. If one CRT is set up to cover whole number subtraction, there has to be a compromise that could lead to some of the criteria being missed out. There has to be a balance between the demands associated with precision and the time available for intervention, whether for teaching or for testing. Such detail as in the full list would result in precision teaching or precision diagnosis. Personal experience of trying out this approach for teaching tells me that it does not lead to rapid progress or catch-up (see also Chapter 10 on cognitive style). Making a specific intervention too lengthy may result in the student losing track of the process. An overview and review may help, but so might a careful 'editing' of the steps.

Whole number subtraction (Ashlock et al., 1983):

1 Basic facts with minuends to 10
2 Basic facts with minuends from 11 to 18
3 Facts with zero as remainder
4 Facts with zero as subtrahend

$$\left.\begin{array}{l} 485 \leftarrow \text{minuend} \\ \underline{-142} \leftarrow \text{subtrahend} \\ 343 \leftarrow \text{remainder} \end{array}\right\}$$

5 Two place minus one place, no ones in remainder, 68 – 8
6 Tens minus tens, 80 – 60
7 Subtraction by endings, no bridging, 28 – 5
8 Two place minus two place, no regrouping, 38 – 22
9 Checking
10 Regrouping tens, 62 – 38
11 Bridging a multiple of ten, 33 – 5
12 Three place minus two place, no regrouping, 365 – 43
13 Hundreds minus hundreds, 900 – 700
14 Three place minus three place, no ones in three-place remainder, 387 – 267
15 Three place minus three place, three-place remainder, no regrouping, 593 – 471
16 Three place minus two place, regrouping a ten, 491 – 98
17 Three place minus two place, regrouping a hundred, 539 – 83
18 Three place minus three place, regrouping a ten, 972 –347
19 Regrouping hundreds, 628 – 437
20 Regrouping a ten and a hundred, 736 – 587
21 Regrouping a thousand, 3570 – 1850
22 Three place minus three place, zero in tens place in minuend, 704 – 375
23 Zero in ones and tens place in minuend, 500 – 284
24 Four place minus four place, zeros in minuend, 3000 – 1346

A selective, edited criterion test for whole number subtraction might look like (criterion in brackets):

16 – 7 =   (2)   26 – 6 =   (5)

$$\begin{array}{r} 84 \\ \underline{-47} \end{array} \ (10) \qquad \begin{array}{r} 142 \\ \underline{-66} \end{array} \ (16)$$

$$\begin{array}{r} 703 \\ \underline{-226} \end{array} \ (22) \qquad \begin{array}{r} 9001 \\ \underline{-2149} \end{array} \ (24)$$

This shortened test only offers one question for each criterion. A correct answer may be more down to luck than expertise, an incorrect answer may be down to a careless error, so the test could be expanded to two items per criterion. The relevant questions here are, 'How much information do you need to be certain? Can you be certain?'

The items are set up to test for the occurrence of predictable errors (see Chapter 9). This is not an attempt to make students fail, but to diagnose, to find evidence that concepts are understood … or not. For example:

16 – 7 is a basic fact that may be retrieved from memory, may be linked to 8 + 8, may be counted back or counted on.

26 – 6 adds in a tens digit to a units subtraction. An answer of 2 would suggest very poor understanding of tens and units (place value).

84 – 47 sets up the 'take the little from the big' error.

142 – 66 demands regrouping/renaming in units and tens … or a double use of the 'little from the big' error, thus providing further evidence of a weak grasp of the concept of decomposing numbers.

703 – 226 introduces a zero which can create its own errors, primarily 0 – 2 = 0 and 0 – 2 = 2, in addition to the renaming error. The idea of regrouping from the hundreds and through the tens in one procedure is an additional layer of complication for many students. There will be many potential errors here, including 523, 503, 427 and 407.

9001– 2149. It should be possible now, using the examples above, to work out what potential errors may be generated by this example.

As with all marking for error diagnosis, it is not that the question is simply 'wrong', but which wrong answer has been given and the misconceptions behind it.

It may be that the decision is to test all of the stages for whole number subtraction, not in one test, but by constructing additional tests that are more focused on each stage. For example, setting up three tests, each focused on eight stages.

One of the findings from the National (US) Advisory Panel (2008) was that testing aids learning by requiring the recall of content-related information. This is unlikely to be true for all students, of course, but, if the testing can be made a positive experience for as many students as possible, then it can become an important part of learning. As ever, the experience of success is motivating.

Setting up CRTs

It may take a while to set up a resource base of CRTs, worksheets and homework sheets, but the outcomes may justify the time taken. If students are going to spend time doing such sheets and teachers are going to spend time marking them, then it seems pragmatic to make those sheets worthwhile for both parties. It makes sense to extract the maximum benefits from work, starting by asking what information you expect to obtain from each question, from selected combinations of questions and from the whole sheet (for example, can you set up items that reveal certain error patterns?) A CRT can focus on common misconceptions and error patterns.

Criteria and objectives

Ashlock et al.'s 24 criteria for whole number subtraction show that the development of this topic has been analysed carefully and thoroughly. Where this is not available, a detailed curriculum may provide much of the information needed to define progression. There is a link between criteria and objectives, if the objectives are specific enough. Broad objectives and goals do not offer the guidance to set up a CRT, for example, 'understand the nature of the four operations and apply them appropriately' or 'add and subtract, with and without renaming, within 9999'.

Pre-requisite skills and knowledge

Any topic in mathematics demands pre-requisite skills and knowledge. *The Trouble with Maths* explores this issue in Chapters 3 and 5 (Chinn, 2012). The knowledge of pre-requisites should help to make the construction and marking of exercises more diagnostic. For example, is the wrong answer in a long multiplication caused by inaccurate recall of basic facts, uncertainty about place value, poor organisation of work on paper or poor addition skills? Questions can be constructed to expose these problems or to eliminate them thus focusing in on a specific facet, for example, item 33 on the 15 minute mathematics test (Chapter 8) is about multiplication. The basic multiplication facts that are involved are for 2 and 3 (541×203), so that the question is more about the procedure used and less about retrieval of basic facts.

A CRT can be constructed to explore developmental factors and pre-requisite skills. For example, a problem with algebra may be rooted in a failure to link back to basic arithmetic. This may be revealed by using questions such as:

$8 + 5 = \boxed{}$ $7 + 9 = y$ Find y

$12 - \boxed{} = 6$ $17 - b = 10$ Find b

Algebra questions do not have to be just about algebra.

Focused CRTs

It may be appropriate to focus on an aspect of a topic, for example, subtraction when zeros are involved.

Subtraction with zeros

1) 10
    $\underline{-4}$

2) 60
    $\underline{-7}$

3) 430
    $\underline{-218}$

4) 200
    $\underline{-4}$

5) 900
    $\underline{-30}$

6) 706
    $\underline{-39}$

7)   400   8)   801
      −218   −510

9)   382   10)   2000
      −102   −672

Number bonds for 10:

0   1   2   3   4   **5**   6   7   8   9   10
10 9   8   7   6   **5**   4   3   2   1   0

Subtraction with zeros: criteria

   1 Ten minus unit (number bond for 10).
   2 Tens minus unit.
   3 Three digit with zero in unit minus three digit, renaming tens.
   4 Hundreds minus units.
   5 Hundreds minus tens.
   6 Three digit with zero in tens, minus two digit, renaming hundreds.
   7 Hundreds minus three digit, renaming in hundreds and tens.
   8 Three digit, zero in tens, minus three digit, zero in units, renaming in hundreds.
   9 Three digit minus three digit, zero in tens, no renaming. Answer has zero in units.
10 Thousands minus three digit, renaming in thousands, hundreds and ten.

NOTE: the number bonds for ten have been given at the bottom of the test. The test is about understanding zero, not about recall of basic facts. The same principle could be applied by providing a multiplication fact square for CRTs on division and multiplication procedures.

   Of course, not every item in every worksheet or test has to be part of a criterion-referenced plan.

Overview CRTs

If the assessment/diagnostic goal is to find out what a person can and cannot do, rather than compare their performance to their peers, then a CRT can be designed to cover a broader range of criteria. In the example below there is only one item per criterion, so it may be helpful to check incorrect answers with a further, similar example. Clinical and empathetic questioning can reveal more information about misconceptions, or more detailed and focused CRTs can be used as a follow-up.

   This test is designed for older learners and adults.

Arithmetic

1) $9 + 8 =$ ___   2) $5 + 8 = 8 +$ ___

3)   79
     +67

4)   308
     +582

5)   142
    −36

6)   703
    −226

7) $17 \times 20 =$ ___

8) $213 \times 105 =$ ___

9) $59 \div 2 =$ ___

10) $10\overline{)4520}$

11) $14.6 - 3 =$ ___

12) $6 - 0.7 =$ ___

13) £26.45 − £5 = ___

14) £10 − 95p= ___

15) $6 \times 7 = 7 \times$ ☐

16) $5 + 5 + 5 + 5 + 5 + 5 =$ ☐ $\times 5$

17) $\dfrac{1}{2} + \dfrac{1}{2} =$ ☐

18) $\dfrac{2}{5} \times 100 =$ ☐

19) $\dfrac{2}{5} + \dfrac{1}{5} =$ ☐

Arithmetic: criteria

1 Single digit plus single digit. A basic fact. (Could be solved by a number of strategies as well as by recall).
2 A test of the commutative property of addition.
3 Two digit minus two digit, no renaming.
4 Three digit plus three digit, carrying from the units, zero in a tens addend.
5 Three digit minus two digit, renaming in the tens.
6 Three digit minus three digit, renaming in tens and hundreds. Zero in tens minuend.
7 Two digit times tens.
8 Three digit times three digit. Zero in tens of multiplier.
9 Two digit divided by one digit with remainder or decimal answer.
10 Four digit with zero in units divided by ten.
11 Decimal with tenths minus whole number.
12 Single digit whole number minus tenths.
13 Two digit pounds and two digit pence minus whole pounds.
14 Two digit pounds minus two digit pence.
15 A test of the commutative property of multiplication.
16 Knowing that repeated addition is multiplication.

17 Fraction plus fraction (same denominator). Everyday example.
18 Fraction times 100.
19 Fraction plus fraction, same denominator.

As always, answers should not just be judged as 'right' or 'wrong'. Errors should be analysed and interpreted where possible and their implications addressed. Correct answers can, of course, often be achieved by more than one route, so it is worth asking about those, too.

Practice may not make perfect

A final note, there is an inherent danger in worksheets and homework sheets. The research dates from 1925 (Buswell and Judd). The cautionary message is based on their observation about the experience of learning something for the first time. If what the person learns is not correct, the brain still learns it. So, incorrect practice is teaching the brain to be wrong. This first learning experience tends to be a dominant one and one that will recur even after attempts to remediate the problem.

Ideally the first two questions of any worksheet or homework need to be checked before the rest are attempted. If the answers are incorrect, it is probably safer not to continue, unless intervention can address the problem before the remaining questions are attempted.

14 Speed of working: The implications of 'doing maths' quickly

Speed of working and speed of responding to questions are part of the culture of mathematics. For example, Bryant et al. (2000) in a survey in the USA of teacher-identified mathematics weaknesses gave, 'Takes a long time to complete calculations' as the sixth ranked weakness (out of 33). There are some further implications and consequences for the learner here, for example, the demand to do something quickly that you find difficult (even when doing it slowly) can make the learner anxious and less effective. It may also encourage the learner to be impulsive and careless.

> It makes mathematics a deal easier and quicker if you know your times tables, but some slower kids are very clever and a good mathematics teacher doesn't equate quickness with ability.
>
> *(Johnston-Wilder, 2008)*

Against this culture of speed of responding there is the issue that slow processing is a characteristic of several learning difficulties, including dyslexia and dyspraxia.

Report from a learning support assistant on a 13-year-old girl. Extract 1:

> Mrs Smith paces the lessons very well and Ellie should be able to follow what she is teaching.

So, there can be inherent reasons, characteristic of a special need or disability, for being a slow processor, but it may also be an indirect consequence of other factors, such as not being able to retrieve facts quickly from memory or a tendency to embark on longer routes towards obtaining answers, for example, a reliance on counting. Sometimes slowness may be down to avoidance.

Learning assistant report. Extract 2:

> I am constantly having to prompt her to look at Mrs Smith and listen to her. She seems to spend a lot of time rubbing out and sharpening her pencil!

As with so many of the learning factors considered in this book, speed of working and slow processing interacts with other factors, creating a variety of combinations of difficulties and thus profiles of learning.

Slow processing, speed of working and examinations

The slower processing speeds of students with special needs are recognised by many examination boards in the UK and other countries. Extra time is one of the less contentious provisions for students with special needs, but it is still likely and reasonable that any request to an Examination Board for extra time will have to be backed by evidence.

This could be direct, specifically obtained evidence, but also it could consist of accumulated evidence. For example, in school or college, whenever a student is given a class-designed test or a standardised test, extra time can be allocated if appropriate and possible. One possibility for gathering evidence would be to change the pen, giving a pen with a different colour ink for the extra time. This should give some indication, from a collection of instances, of the impact of extra time on scores.

A previous study

In a classroom study (Chinn, 1995), 21 items were used to compare the working times of dyslexic and mainstream students aged 11 to 13 years. The multiplication and division items were selected to avoid number facts that are often less readily available to dyslexic students, that is × and ÷ by 6, 7, 8 and 9. The items were:

16 + 37	308 +897	12.3 + 5	19.09 + 10.91	63 + 2.1
67 − 32	72 − 48	813 −668	601 −346	37.6 − 4 21.03 −2.14
5 × 6	5 × 60	33 × 20	44 × 21	25 × 202
2)39̄	6040 ÷ 10	3)9̄0̄6̄	5)6̄6̄8̄	15)3̄4̄5̄

The sample was 122 dyslexic pupils, 11–13-years-old, from eight specialist schools for dyslexic students and 122 pupils from the upper sets of nine mainstream schools.

The results for time taken to finish working on the test were:

Dyslexic pupils – 13.00 min, SD 5.41
Mainstream pupils – 8.50 min, SD 3.41 (but see below)

The scores for the two groups (out of 21) were:

Dyslexic pupils – 10.1, SD 5.6
Mainstream – 15.6, SD 4.1

But there is a problem with this data …

The 'no answer'

This 1995 classroom study was set up primarily to investigate and compare error patterns made by mainstream students and dyslexic students. However, the test did provide some preliminary data on speed of working and accuracy as shown above. The results would seem to suggest that dyslexic students took, on average, about 50 per cent more time to complete this task than their mainstream peers. However, there is a significant caution, based on the error patterns exhibited by the two groups. The students with dyslexia showed far more blanks, 'no answers', in their scripts. The evidence from the study was that the 'Don't think I can get this correct, so I won't try' strategy was more far, far more frequently used by students with dyslexia.

The implication for evaluation is, therefore, to consider the number of items that were not attempted. However, the impact of this on the time taken to perform the test is not quantifiable. It does make any direct measurement of speed of working more challenging and should make the interpretation of attempts to measure speed of working directly more cautious.

The trials on using this test for the current protocol indicated that the 'no answer' issue made comparisons unreliable. Some subjects answered all the questions, some only attempted a few. The test was not comparing the same tasks and was, therefore, abandoned.

This is not a problem for evaluating writing speed, where subjects can be asked to write freely or copy, rather than be involved in decisions about whether or not a question can be answered.

Indirect evidence

The evidence for slow processing can be collected and inferred from other tests. The basic fact tests are a possible indicator of slow processing, particularly the addition and subtraction tests. The results from the standardising data showed that subjects made few errors on the addition and subtraction tests. It was the number of answers attempted that was the major contributing factor to the score.

Similarly, the 15 minute mathematics test provides evidence of slow work. If the score is low primarily because the number of items attempted is low, rather than a large number of errors, then the cause is likely to be slow processing.

Accumulated evidence is likely to be most reliable.

15 Two sample reports

Mathematics assessment/diagnosis
Steve Chinn, BSc, PhD, Dip Ed Man, PGCE, AMBDA
   PRIVATE and CONFIDENTIAL
Name: Sally
School: The Big Academy
DOB: XX.02.01
Date of assessment: 10.06.2011
Age at assessment: 10y 4m

Psychologist's report

Not available.

The assessment

This assessment is designed to investigate the areas of maths which are causing concern and those that are contributing to difficulties. It is also looking at areas of strength. Primarily it is a clinical assessment.

Sally applied herself to the tasks well for just over one hour. She did write with her head close to the paper. She said that her eyes get tired especially when staring at the board too much. I would also speculate that her very weak working memory would require her to focus on the board, focus on the paper, back to the board and so on, creating tiredness. It would be worth having her vision checked.

Main concerns

Parents

Sally struggles with basic maths and has problems with number bonds. There are also memory problems and problems with processing information.

School concerns

Sally's school report says that maths is a cause for concern and her lower level of achievement stands out in comparison to other subjects.

Sally's comments

What do you like best in maths?

'Times tables. Addition and subtraction. I like working things out in my head.'

What do you like least?

'Division.' Sally finds some explanations of maths ideas are not clear for her.

The Dyscalculia Checklist

The Checklist was filled in before the session. The Checklist could be used to help the structure of an individual education plan for Sally. The characteristics in the Checklist are influential on how children learn and progress through maths.

Does the learner ....

1 Have difficulty counting objects accurately. ☐

2 Lack the ability to make 'one to one correspondence' when counting (match the number to the object) ☐

3 Find it impossible to 'see' that four objects are 4 without counting (or 3, if a young child) ☐

4 Write 51 for fifteen or 61 for sixteen (and all teen numbers) ☐

5 Have difficulty remembering addition facts   X

6 Count on for addition facts, as for 7 + 3, counting on 8, 9, 10 to get your answer ☐

7 Count all the numbers when adding, as for 7 + 3 again, you count 1,2,3,4,5,6,7,8,9,10 ☐

8 Not 'see' immediately that 7 + 5 is the same as 5 + 7 or that 7 × 3 is the same as 3 × 7   X

9 Use tally marks for addition or subtraction problems ☐

10 Find it difficult to progress from using materials (fingers, blocks, tallies) to using only numbers ☐

11 Find it much harder to count backwards compared to forwards   X

12 Find it difficult to count fluently less familiar sequences, such as: 1,3,5,7,9,11 … or 14,24,34,44,54,64 … ☐

13 Only know the 2 ×, 5 × and 10 multiplication facts ☐

14 Count on to access the 2 × and 5 × facts ☐

15 Able to learn the other basic multiplication facts, but then forget them overnight   *Until 4 weeks ago*

16 Make 'big' errors for multiplication facts, such as 6 × 7 = 67 or 6 × 7 = 13   *in recent past*

17 Find it difficult to write numbers which have zeros within them, such as 'four thousand and twenty one'   *sometimes*

18 Find it difficult to judge whether an answer is right, or nearly right   X

19 Find estimating impossible   X

20 Struggle with mental arithmetic   X

21 'See' numbers literally and not inter-related, for example, do you count from
     1 to get 9, rather than subtracting 1 away from 10   X
22 Forget the question asked in mental arithmetic   X
23 Prefer to use formulas (when you remember them!), but use them
     mechanically without any understanding of how they work   X
24 Forget mathematical procedures, especially as they become more
     complex, such as decomposing or borrowing for subtraction and
     almost certainly any method for division   X
25 Think that algebra is impossible to understand   X
26 Organise your written work poorly, for example you do not line
     up columns of numbers properly   *sometimes*
27 Have poor skills with money, for example, are you unable to calculate
     change from a purchase   X
28 Think an item priced at £4.99 is '£4 and a bit' rather than almost £5   ☐
29 Not see and pick up patterns or generalisations, especially ones
     that are new to you, for example that 1/2, 1/3, 1/4, 1/5 is a sequence
     that is getting smaller   ☐
30 Get very anxious about doing ANY maths   X
31 Refuse to try any maths, especially unfamiliar topics   ☐
32 Become impulsive when doing maths, rather than being analytical.
     Do you rush to get it over with?   X

These items provide an initial picture of Sally's difficulties. These include a problem with remembering the basic facts (see later), counting backwards, which can be the precursor skill for subtraction and a sense of number values as used in estimating or inter-relating numbers.

The session

Coins

I spread a number of coins (27) over the table and asked Sally to guess how many were there. This exercise is low stress and explores sense of number.

Sally estimated 44.

I asked Sally to count the coins. She did this accurately and quickly.

I gave Sally 21 1p coins and three 10p coins. I asked her to give me 9p. She counted them out. I asked again and Sally gave me 9 1p coins. I asked again and Sally viewed the 3p left and paused for a while. She knew that she could hand me a 10p coin and ask for 1p back, but was interpreting what I had asked literally. Once I allowed her to be 'creative' she was fine.

Dots on a card

I asked Sally to estimate the number of dots randomly organised on a card. She answered 7. I asked her to count them, which she did accurately as 13.

Then I showed her 11 dots in a line. Her estimate was 12 and her count was 11. (See also Thinking Style, below.)

It would be productive to spend some time on low-stress exercises that develop number sense.

Basic facts: introductory exercises

This series of tasks is examining number facts, whether they are retrieved from memory or counted or accessed by strategies.

4 2 Answer 4. 'I just know.'

3 6 Answer 9. 'I just know.'

5 + __ = 9 Again Sally knew the answer quickly, adapting to the different presentation.

7 + 6 Sally linked this fact to 8 + 5.

10 + 7 Very quick response of 17. Followed this with **9 + 7** and Sally quickly answered 17. I showed Sally both fact cards together and she changed her answer to 16.

We talked about another example of this idea, adding 100 + 26 and then 99 + 26. Sally was able to work out the link. This is a skill to develop.

60 – 7 Sally sub-vocalised (a good learning skill) and answered hesitantly, '54'. She is not linking in the number bonds for 10 here (see later).

5 + 6 Sally says that sometimes she knows that this is 11 and sometimes she links it to 5 + 5.

14 × 2 A slow response and then a hesitant '28' achieved by adding 14 to 14.

14 × 20 '63, just a guess' Sally tried to explain more, but her method was very confused.

These items explore Sally's knowledge of facts and her use of, and potential to use linking strategies when retrieval fails. It would be beneficial to work on place value concepts, including multiplying and dividing by ten and powers of ten. This could be a key approach for Sally and her teachers.

Place value cards 56, 371, 8572, 14273

Sally was secure and accurate reading numbers to four figures, thousands, but insecure beyond this.

Number bonds for 10

I asked Sally to write two numbers which add to make 10. The number bonds for 10 are key facts and can be extended used extensively in arithmetic. The task reveals the use of patterns/sequences and the commutative property of addition facts.

Sally's sequence of answers was:

9 + 1, 5 + 5, 8 + 2, 7 + 3, 6 + 4, 0 + 10. She paused and asked if she could write them the other way around, then continued 1 + 9, 2 + 8, 3 + 7 ...

Sally's father has been teaching her the patterns and the commutative property and Sally has learned well. Patterns can be a great help when a child has a weak memory for maths facts and procedures.

We talked about some of the applications of these facts and again Sally showed that she could adapt to these ideas.

Basic facts: 60 second/120 second worksheets

These four separate tests measure retrieval of basic facts for the four operations (+ − × ÷) using a relatively low stress approach. Poor retrieval of these basic facts is frequently quoted in research into maths learning difficulties as a major contributing factor to low achievement.

Facts may be retrieval from memory or retrieved via strategies. The most basic strategy is counting, often using fingers. More sophisticated strategies link facts, for example, 6 + 5 as 5 + 5 + 1. The major research survey of Hattie (2009) concluded that strategy based methods are one of the most effective interventions in education.

Sally's scores were:

Addition: 11/36 Av 24, SD 7.3. Sally's score is almost 2 SD below the mean.
Subtraction: 14/36 Av 22.5, SD 8.4. Sally's score is more than 1 SD below the mean.
Multiplication: 22/36 Av 26.5, SD 9.0 Sally's score is just above the 25th percentile.
Division: 15/33 Av 21.5, SD 10.4. Sally's score is at the 25th percentile.

Sally's answers for the addition facts were all correct. Her low score was down to slow processing (largely due to finger counting).

For the subtraction facts, all correct again, but slow.

For the multiplication facts Sally made 4 wrong answers out of 26. Her relatively high score on this task must be down to many hours of practice. Her errors are 'mismatches', for example, 8 × 4 = 36 and 4 × 8 = 24.

For the division facts Sally made six errors (and answered correctly 24 ÷ 3). These included 2 ÷ 1 = 1 and 4 ÷ 1 = 1, a not uncommon conceptual error.

Sally needs to learn strategies which will help her retrieve these facts and also help her to build the foundations for many maths concepts, such as 'long' multiplication.

Short-term memory, working memory

Working memory is correlated to maths ability in many research papers. Also it has been shown that working memory is weakened by anxiety. Short-term memory affects the ability to remember instructions.

These skills were tested by using a digits-forward and digits-reversed test.

Sally can manage five items forwards, but struggles with three items reversed. This is when she is focusing just on the task, not when it is a part of other processing, so this has to be considered as a very significant handicap for Sally. It is going to be very beneficial (probably crucial to her ability to absorb information in class) for information to be repeated for Sally, for information to be given in small chunks, or handouts supplied or a 'buddy' used to help her start tasks. Mental arithmetic is likely to be a difficulty as a consequence of her weak working memory.

Symbols and words

This is a task where Sally had to match the word to the symbol, for example, 'share' and ÷, by sorting a collection of word cards under each of the four operation symbols.

Sally matched most cards, but placed 'share' under + and 'of' under ÷.

Anxiety

Sally and I talked through the 20 items in the questionnaire used in my research into maths anxiety.

Anxiety is exacerbated by the fear of failure. Avoidance is one strategy pupils use to deal with this (as do adults). Among the many consequences is apparent lack of attention.

Sally only ranked one item as 'always creates anxiety', the 'end of term maths test'. She ranked 'Revising for a maths test', 'Working out money when shopping', 'Looking at marks for homework' and 'Following your teacher's explanation of a new topic' as 'often creates anxiety'.

Thinking style

This exercise is based on *The Test of Cognitive Style in Mathematics* by Bath, Chinn and Knox and published by Slosson in the USA in 1986.

Sally was given a number of maths items and asked to explain how she worked out her answers.

There are two cognitive styles. Most people use a mixture of both. Learners who are at either extreme of this spectrum are at risk. In particular the 'Inchworm' procedural, literal style student who also has poor working memory and poor long-term mathematical memory is at risk. The intuitive 'Grasshopper', who has good sense of number and an understanding of the four operations and their interrelationships is often good at estimation and mental arithmetic, but is at risk in maths because 'Grasshoppers' tend not to document their methods. Ideally learners need to be able to use both styles and at appropriate times when problem solving.

I asked Sally to try four items from the test. Sally can understand some of the Grasshopper skills for number work, skills that will help her develop a stronger sense of number and introduce a more flexible approach to maths processes. On the question which presents a grid of 49 alternately black and white 49 squares Sally's initial estimate of 'How many black squares?' was (an impressive estimate) 24.

These exercises show that on computation questions Sally should be encouraged to estimate and to appraise the estimate using, 'Is it bigger or smaller?'

WRAT-IV: The Wide Range Achievement Test

This 15 minute (maximum) test was designed and standardised in the USA. It makes a useful screener. It gives an indication of the level of achievement. There are no word problems in the WRAT, so it is essentially language free.

Sally's score put her at the 42 percentile, but these are USA norms for a USA test, so this percentile has to be treated with some caution.

Sally showed great perseverance and application with the test, working through to the end despite the latter items being challenging for a 10-year-old. Item 37 asks the subject to 'Evaluate' and Sally said she had forgotten what evaluate meant. This is a reminder that even low language content tests make some language demands. Sally needs input for vocabulary and language issues.

Her errors reveal some clues about her concepts and use of procedures, for example:

$$\begin{array}{r} 46 \\ -29 \\ \hline 23 \end{array}$$

where Sally took the 'little from the big' number in the units column

Item 15. 1½ hour = 65 min. The use of base 60 often confuses learners. Interventions for issues with time are a good example of the need to take the learner back to fundamentals.

Item 17.

$$\begin{array}{r} 34 \\ \times 21 \\ \hline 64 \end{array}$$

where Sally used a logical, but incorrect procedure. This error could also reveal a problem with applying place value concepts.

Item 18. ¾ = 34% Again, intervention needs to go back to basic concepts.

I was impressed with Sally's correct procedure with Item 16.

$$\begin{array}{r} 401 \\ -74 \\ \hline \end{array}$$

where she carried out the renaming correctly. This is not often the case.

Sally does have areas of strength that can be used to build confidence and to develop other maths skills.

Summary

Sally worked hard and with good humour throughout the assessment. She is an able girl who needs to be shown the links, patterns and concepts of maths. Her issues with memory, short, working and long, will handicap her learning, not her ability. These factors need to be addressed at all times for her, by repeating information, presenting it visually and orally, maybe giving her table squares when learning long multiplication and division procedures. There are other suggestions within the body of this report.

Sally retains motivation and application. I think that she needs and deserves more experience of success to sustain this attitude.

Mathematics assessment/diagnosis
Steve Chinn, BSc, PhD, Dip Ed Man, PGCE, AMBDA
   PRIVATE and CONFIDENTIAL
Name: Amie
School: The Caring School
DOB: XX.03.2000
Date of assessment: 11.05.2011
Age at assessment: 11y 2m
Referred by: Father

Speech and language therapy report

Amie's father provided me with a copy of this report carried out on 22/01/2010. Amie's spelling age as assessed with the SWST was at the 7th percentile, 3 years below her chronological age.

Amie's auditory memory at age 9y 10m was 8y 6m for forward digits (short-term memory) and 7y 11m for backwards digits (working memory).

Informal testing showed that Amie was not able to complete all the (maths) targets expected of a child at the end of Year 4.

Informal assessment showed that Amie is of an average to high average intellectual potential.

The assessment

This assessment is designed to investigate the areas of maths which are causing concern and those that are contributing to difficulties. It is also looking at areas of strength. Primarily it is a clinical assessment.

Main concerns

Parents

'Amie is struggling with the basic elements of formulaic maths. By this I mean that she has difficulty in seeing how the numbers go together in patterns and position. She has developed some coping strategies for small numbers but as things get more complex she ends up at sea.'

'An observation I have made is that she approaches things in a very creative way and maths is no different in her thoughts. Therefore interpretation without formula results in errors. This frustrates her.'

'She seems constantly tired and with the additional problems of homework life is hard for Amie.'

Teacher concerns

Keeping up in class as well as knowing tables and arithmetic problems in order to move forward into more complex maths.

Amie's comments

What do you like best in maths? What do you like least?

Amie gave a lot of thought to her answers. 'I don't like division. I'm OK at times tables. I don't like adding columns ... and that's the other thing ... I'm not good at money. Fractions. I'm not very good at word problems.'

I asked Amie to rank herself on a scale of 1 to 10 to grade how good she feels she is at maths. Amie's response was 'Probably 6 or 7'

These comments combine well with Amie's responses to the Anxiety Questionnaire.

The Dyscalculia Checklist

The Checklist was filled in before the session. The items were graded as:

   1 not a big problem 2 some problem caused 3 a big problem

The Checklist can be used to help the structure of an individual education plan for Amie. The characteristics in the Checklist are influential on how children learn and progress through maths.

Hattie's (2009) review of research into what is effective in education found that discussing problems with the child is one of the most effective strategies.

Does the learner ....

1 Have difficulty counting objects accurately	1
2 Lack the ability to make 'one to one correspondence' when counting (match the number to the object)	1
3 Find it impossible to 'see' that four objects are 4 without counting (or 3, if a young child)	1
4 Write 51 for fifteen or 61 for sixteen (and all teen numbers)	1
5 Have difficulty remembering addition facts	3
6 Count on for addition facts, as for 7 + 3, counting on 8, 9, 10 to get your answer	2
7 Count all the numbers when adding, as for 7 + 3 again, you count 1,2,3,4,5,6,7,8,9,10	1
8 Not 'see' immediately that 7 + 5 is the same as 5 + 7 or that 7×3 is the same as 3×7	2
9 Use tally marks for addition or subtraction problems	1
10 Find it difficult to progress from using materials (fingers, blocks, tallies) to using only numbers	3
11 Find it much harder to count backwards compared to forwards	3
12 Find it difficult to count fluently less familiar sequences, such as: 1,3,5,7,9,11 ... or 14,24,34,44,54,64 ...	3
13 Only know the 2 ×, 5 × and 10 multiplication facts	3 (inc 4 ×)
14 Count on to access the 2 × and 5 × facts	3
15 Able to learn the other basic multiplication facts, but then forget them overnight	2

16 Make 'big' errors for multiplication facts, such as $6 \times 7 = 67$ or $6 \times 7 = 13$ 1

17 Find it difficult to write numbers which have zeros within them, such as
   'four thousand and twenty one'   2

18 Find it difficult to judge whether an answer is right, or nearly right   2

19 Find estimating impossible   2

20 Struggle with mental arithmetic   3

21 'See' numbers literally and not inter-related, for example, do you count
   from 1 to get 9, rather than subtracting 1 away from 10   3

22 Forget the question asked in mental arithmetic   3

23 Prefer to use formulas (when you remember them!), but use them
   mechanically without any understanding of how they work   3

24 Forget mathematical procedures, especially as they become more complex,
   such as decomposing or borrowing for subtraction and almost certainly
   any method for division   3

25 Think that algebra is impossible to understand   3

26 Organise your written work poorly, for example you do not line up columns
   of numbers properly   2

27 Have poor skills with money, for example, are you unable to calculate
   change from a purchase   3

28 Think an item priced at £4.99 is '£4 and a bit' rather than almost £5   3

29 Not see and pick up patterns or generalisations, especially ones that
   are new to you, for example that 1/2, 1/3, 1/4, 1/5 is a sequence that
   is getting smaller   2

30 Get very anxious about doing ANY maths   3

31 Refuse to try any maths, especially unfamiliar topics   2

32 Become impulsive when doing maths, rather than being analytical.
   Do you rush to get it over with?   1

Although most of these items are self explanatory, I have focused on some of the key issues that they reveal.

Item 22. Amie has a weak short term memory and will find it difficult to remember complex questions. Repeating them may help. Showing them will be better. Mental arithmetic makes demands that require differentiation for students such as Amie.

Item 20. Amie's poor stm and her weak working memory will combine to make mental arithmetic very difficult. A further factor will be her poor retrieval of basic facts. If lessons begin with mental arithmetic then Amie will not start maths with a positive experience of success.

Items 5, 6, 8, 13, 14 and 15. According to my informal research when working with teachers, the percentage of children to whom these issues apply is very high. They are highly significant and frequent for pupils with dyslexia. It is nothing to do with the effort a pupil puts into trying to rote learn the facts. For reasons which are not yet researched (neurologists do not have the technology as yet), it is the situation. There are strategies that can be taught to help. These strategies can also help with the understanding of maths concepts. (See 'The Trouble with Maths' and 'What to do when you can't learn the times tables', both by Steve Chinn.)

It is likely that continued attempts to use only rote learning for all these facts will be de-motivating.

Note in Item 16 that Amie does not make big errors for times table facts. This suggests that she has some sense of number.

Items 18, 19, 21 and 28 are about number sense and also the tendency for some pupils to see numbers literally and not linked to other numbers. Each fact is seen in isolation creating huge memory demands.

Item 17 is about place value, a sophisticated concept which permeates arithmetic. I would also want to check its influence on 'long' multiplication and subtraction procedures.

Item 11. Maths starts with counting. Children who find counting backwards a problem may not have set the foundations for understanding subtraction. They may not link this operation to addition and may not, therefore, link any of the four operations. This will severely handicap any understanding and thus ability to recall procedures.

Item 12. If patterns and sequences can be recognised then memory will be supported and pupils will also develop the skills of generalising.

Items 23 and 24. Even though many children find formulas difficult to remember accurately, they continue to use them basing this choice on a false sense of security.

The session

Coins and dots

I spread a number of coins (47) over the table and asked Amie to guess how many were there. Her estimate was 20. This exercise is low stress and explores sense of number.

I asked her to count the coins. Amie was quick and accurate in her counting. She counted in ones and did not group the coins. I showed Amie how to group in fives, using the card/dice pattern, and thus tens. She understood and took to the idea. Exercises like this help to build number sense.

I asked Amie to estimate and then count some randomly arranged dots on a card (13). Her estimate was 12 and her counting, accurate, was 12. Then dots in a line where Amie's estimate and count (11) were accurate. These exercises suggest that Amie's number sense at these levels is good. Thus further work on comparing numbers such as 9 and 10 could be approached this way and thus introducing place value as a revision topic. For example, I gave Amie about 23 1p coins and two 10p coins and asked her to give me 9p and then again. When she ran out of enough 1p coins I asked her for another 9p. After a short pause she offered a 10p coin and asked for 1p back. There are several ideas that could be taught from this exercise, including estimates, 'bigger or smaller' and place value.

Basic facts: introductory exercises

This series of tasks is examining number facts, whether they are retrieved from memory or counted or accessed by 'linking' strategies.

The section starts with numbers on cards.

4 2 what do these add to make? Amie answered 6, a slow response. She 'just knows' this fact.

3 6 '9' was quite quick. Amie used her fingers, but she did start with 6

5 + __ = 9 '4' via 5 + 5, showing an ability to link facts.
10 + 7 '17' was quick and Amie 'just knew'.
9 + 7 '16' was linked to 10 + 7.
(Amie began to fiddle with her sleeves, so some anxiety/discomfort here.)

On some place value tasks, Amie was successful, but slow and uncertain (see also later comments). It is a concept that needs securing.

On the series task of **2 4 6 _ 10 12** Amie was quick to answer 8.
On **3 6 9 _** she again was quick to answer 12.
On **91 82 73 _** she hesitantly asked, 'Is it 64?'

This suggests that Amie can deal with sequences and patterns and that this could be used in developing her number sense.

Number bonds for 10

I asked Amie to write two numbers which add to make 10. The number bonds for 10 are key facts and can be used extensively in arithmetic. The task reveals the use of patterns/sequences and the commutative property of addition facts.

Amie wrote 4 + 6   3 + 7   5 + 5   9 + 1   8 + 2   2 + 8   7 + 3   6 + 4   1 + 9

Amie recognised the commutative property, but it was not foremost in her mind. This is another example of half known facts and concepts which need to be secured and linked to support her weak memories (short-term, working and long-term). Amie was also able to relate 6 + 5 to 5 + 5. She shows the ability to take key facts and extend them by mathematically sound strategies.

Basic facts: 60 second/120 second worksheets

These four separate tests measure retrieval of basic facts for the four operations (+ − × ÷) using a relatively low stress approach. Poor retrieval of these basic facts is frequently quoted in research into maths learning difficulties as a major contributing factor to low achievement.

Facts may be retrieval from memory or retrieved via strategies. The most basic strategy is counting, often using fingers. More sophisticated strategies link facts, for example, 6 + 5 as 5 + 5 + 1. The major research survey of Hattie (2009) concluded that strategy based methods are one of the most effective interventions in education.

Addition: Amie answered 16 questions, all correctly. The average for her age is 23. Her score placed her between the 10th and 25th percentile. She paused at 6 + 4 even though she had chosen 4 + 6 as her first number bond for 10.

Subtraction: Amie faced this task with a very clear 'Oh no' look on her face. She used finger counting. The 6 − 5 and 8 − 7 items took a while, suggesting that Amie was not using number sense under test conditions. She scored 13, all correct answers. The average for her age is 22. A score of 13 is just above the 10th percentile.

Multiplication: Amie finger counted for the × 2 items. She answered the × 0 items correctly and the × 1 items. Children who are weak at maths often fail on these items.

Successful knowledge such as these items can be used to build up further knowledge. For example, Amie answered 14×2 correctly, then 14×20, though with some uncertainty in her voice, then 14×200, though she struggled to read 2800 correctly, first giving 'two thousand and eighty' Again suggesting work is needed to secure place value concepts. Amie scored 22. All answers were correct. The average for her age is 26. This score is above the 25th percentile.

Division: Amie attempted nine items, getting four correct. She has problems with $\div 1$. This could be a good place to start to address her poor concept of division. The average score for her age is 19. Amie's score was just above the 10th percentile.

Amie's scores on the subtraction and division tests were very low. These 'reverse' operations will need attention. They need to be linked to the 'forward' operations of addition and multiplication where Amie's performance is much stronger.

Word and symbol matching for the four operations

A number of cards, each with a word used for one of the four operations are placed on a table and the pupil is asked to place them under the correct symbol card.

Amie was quite deliberate and somewhat slow in this task, but placed each word correctly, except for 'of' which she placed under $\div$.

Amie's work throughout the session was not fast. It is a characteristic of children with specific (and other) learning difficulties that they process some information slowly. In a maths culture of quick answers, this is a great handicap. It is also a further reason to adjust the quantity, but not the quality, of work demanded of Amie.

Short-term memory, working memory

Working memory is correlated to maths ability in many research papers. Also it has been shown that working memory is weakened by anxiety. Short-term memory affects the ability to remember instructions.

Respected researchers such as Susan Gathercole consider weak working memory as a disability in itself.

These skills were tested by using a digits-forward and digits-reversed test.

Although Amie had done a similar test with her speech therapist, I wanted to see what Amie could do and with what level of security.

Ultimately, Amie could repeat five digits forwards, but that required significant concentration. Unfortunately children are not always in that position when dealing with information in the classroom or when dual tasking.

For digits reversed Amie again concentrated hard and could manage four.

These results illustrate the problems that Amie will have in many aspects of work in the classroom, from instructions to methods taught for mental arithmetic. Instructions may have to repeated and/or chunked into small quantities. Copying work will be slower and more prone to errors. Among other implications is the amount of work that is expected of Amie, for example, a selected number of questions from a work sheet in class or for homework. Over facing Amie will only lead to de-motivation and work she does when tired is likely to be less accurate and assimilated.

Anxiety

Amie and I filled in the questionnaire used in my research into maths anxiety.

Anxiety is exacerbated by the fear of failure. Avoidance is one strategy pupils use to deal with this (as do adults). Among the many consequences is apparent lack of attention. Anxiety also makes working memory less effective (and Amie's working memory is already weak).

Amie gave every question a lot of deliberation. The items which she graded as highest were 'Long division questions without a calculator', 'Working out money when shopping', 'Following explanations of work in class', 'Revising for a maths test', 'Maths homework', 'Learning the hard times table facts' and 'Taking an end of term maths exam'. Thus 7 out of 20 items were ranked as 'often make me anxious'.

Success tends to reduce anxiety and failure increases it, often to the point of withdrawing from the task. Again this suggests that worksheets and homework need to be differentiated for Amie.

Estimation

Estimation follows some different rules to precise calculations and requires a different approach. Good estimation skills show a good sense of number.

See comments under 'Thinking Style' and note the initial coins and dots exercises.

WRAT-IV: The Wide Range Achievement Test

This 15 minute (maximum) test was designed and standardised in the USA. It makes a useful screener. It gives an indication of the level of achievement. There are no word problems in the WRAT, so it is essentially language free.

Amie attempted 25 items and got 14 correct. This put her in the 23rd percentile for her age (USA norms). However, this is not a comprehensive test, but it does not absorb too much assessment time. I know that the score alone does not give an accurate picture. An analysis of the items shows significant gaps in Amie's knowledge of basic maths.

The questions that Amie answered correctly were testing very basic skills. She showed no concept of 2 digit $\times$ 2 digit multiplication ($34 \times 21 = 64$) and made two conceptual errors on $401 - 74$ to get 473. Amie's attempts at two of the division items were a long way from showing any understanding of the processes or concepts. Further examples include Amie asking about a (vertical) subtraction problem, 'In take away sums is it this take away that or that take away that?' (pointing at the numbers at the top and bottom of the subtraction problem). Although 512×3 was correctly answered, Amie did it as 5×3 and then 12×3. After a long time thinking Amie left the rounding question (278 to the nearest ten) unanswered. In question 22, 3)17, Amie asked, 'How many ones are there in three?'

Thinking style

This exercise is based on *The Test of Cognitive Style in Mathematics* by Bath, Chinn and Knox and published by Slosson in the USA in 1986.

There are two cognitive styles. Most people use a mixture of both. Learners who are at either extreme of this spectrum are at risk. In particular the 'Inchworm' procedural, literal style student who also has poor working memory and poor long-term mathematical memory is at risk. The intuitive 'Grasshopper', who has good sense of number and an understanding of the four operations and their inter-relationships is often good at estimation and mental arithmetic, but is at risk in maths because 'Grasshoppers' tend not to document their methods. Ideally learners need to be able to use both styles and at appropriate times when problem solving.

Amie was given a number of maths items from the test and asked to explain how she worked out her answers.

47 + 99 (mental arithmetic) Amie added the units then the tens digits.

I asked what would be an easier number to add instead of the 99 and Amie quickly replied '100', suggesting that she can round numbers. She was also able to work out that after adding 100 she would have to subtract 1.

121 – 99 was 'too hard' (we had been working for quite a while by now and Amie was beginning to tire). We discussed subtracting 100 which was OK, but adjusting by adding back 1 will take a little more explanation. This would be valuable work for Amie from a number of applications, including rounding, estimating and refining an estimate, and appraising by 'Is the (interim) answer bigger or smaller?'

Two shape and space type questions were unsuccessful as Amie was too tired. However I would want to check if she needs more practice in seeing the 'big picture' before starting on the details.

Summary

Amie has far too many gaps in her basic fact retrieval and conceptual understanding to progress in maths. To be blunt, it is likely that she will fall further behind as the curriculum moves on at a far faster pace than she can currently cope with.

Within this report there are observations and comments that are designed to be helpful in planning the intervention that Amie clearly needs.

This intervention has to take account of what helps Amie to learn and remember and what does not work for her (most notably an over-reliance on rote learning).

Her intervention should include time spent in building a deep understanding of the fundamental concepts, for example, how addition relates to subtraction and how division relates to subtraction and to multiplication. Her poor retrieval of facts and procedures should be improved by using her ability to link facts and thus operations.

Appendix 1
A sample 'teacher observations' pro-forma

If the student has input from a support assistant/teacher then it may well be worth obtaining information from both sources.
There will be an underlying reason for each of the behaviours. The diagnostic interview should explore those reasons.

Teacher/tutor observations. Mathematics

Student's name ....   Date ....

Teacher's name .... E-mail ....

School ....

Please rank each item as occurring:

1 never   2 rarely   3 sometimes   4 often   5 always

Please give examples where possible

Does the student.........

☐   Avoid starting work

☐   Have a short attention span

☐   Have a poor/low level of participation in group activities

☐   Lose focus when listening to instructions

☐   Take a long time to respond to oral maths questions

☐   Not concentrate in maths classes ... just not 'there'

☐ Withdraw from or avoid involvement in any maths activities

☐ Take a long time to do worksheets in class

☐ Present written work untidily

☐ Miss out questions on worksheets

☐ Copy work from the board inaccurately

☐ Seem anxious about maths

Have poor and/or slow recall of basic facts:

☐ Addition and subtraction facts

☐ Multiplication and division facts

☐ Avoid and/or fail to answer mental arithmetic questions

☐ Disrupt classes

☐ Hand in homework

Any other comments?

It would be helpful if you could provide a typical example of the student's work

Thank you for taking the time to complete this report.

Appendix 2
A pre-assessment pro-forma for parents/carers

CONFIDENTIAL

Pre-assessment details

Name of child/adult ....Date of Birth ....

Address ....

....

Brothers/sisters (with ages). For school pupils only.

....

Present School plus address or University/College/ employer details

....

....E-mail ....

Year Group. For school pupils only.......................Set (if applicable).............

Parents' (tutor's) main concerns with maths

Adult/Child's main concerns with maths

Any comments from school/University/College regarding maths/numeracy performance

Are there any other areas of concern?

If you have any educational/psychological test reports, it would be useful if I may see these before I assess you/your child.

Signed .... Name .... Date ....

Appendix 3
Schools, colleges, institutions and individuals who provided data for the norm-referenced tests in Chapters 6 and 8

1 Shaw Wood Primary, Armthorpe, Doncaster
2 Sturminster Newton High School, Dorset
3 City College, King's Rd, Devonport, Plymouth
4 Ludlow College, Shropshire
5 Laura Stott and friends
6 Emily and Jamie Chinn and friends
7 City of Bristol College, Brunel Centre, Ashley Down Rd, Bristol
8 Tain Royal Academy, Scotsburn Rd, Tain, Ross-shire
9 The Henry Beaufort School, East Woodhay Rd, Harestock, Winchester
10 City Lit, London
11 Cwm Glas Primary School, Colwyn Ave, Winchwen, Swansea
12 Isle of Man Prison
13 Isle of Man College, Douglas, IoM
14 Stanbridge Earls School, Romsey
15 St Ninian's High School, Douglas, Isle of Man
16 Ballymacrickett Primary School, 41 Scroggy Rd, Glenavy
17 St Joseph's Primary School,15 Glenavy Rd. Crumlim, Co. Antrim
18 Moat Community College, Leicester
19 Sandfield Close Primary School, Leicester
20 St Paul's Secondary School, Evington, Leicester
21 St Barnabas Primary School, Leicester
22 Sir Jonathan North Community College School, Leicester
23 De Ferrers Academy, Burton upon Trent
24 Bishops Stopford School, Headlands, Kettering
25 Hereford Cathedral School
26 Finton House School, London
27 Staffordshire SENSS
28 Truro School, Cornwall
29 Communication Workers Union
30 Edge Hill University, Ormskirk
31 Alison Shorrock
32 Jean Bines, Swansea
33 South Downs College, Waterlooville
34 Grantown Grammar School, Cromdale Rd, Grantown on Spey,
35 Chew Valley School, Chew Magna, Bristol
36 Northfield Academy, Granitehill Place, Aberdeen
37 Logie Durno School, Pitcaple, Inverurie
38 Kingsland CE Primary School, Kingsland, Leominster

39 Milne's High School, West St, Fochabers
40 Coleg Ceredigion, Park Place, Cardigan
41 Truro College, Cornwall
42 St Crispin's School, St Mary's Rd, Leicester
43 Ravenscourt Prep School, Ravenscourt Ave, London
44 Phil Smart, SNIP (Denstone College)
45 Beech Hall School, Tytherington, Macclesfield
46 Dean Close School, Shelburne Rd, Cheltenham
47 King's College, South Rd, Taunton
48 Mayfield School, The Old Palace, Mayfield, E Sussex
49 Alderley Edge School for Girls, Alderley Edge, Cheshire
50 Arnold Lodge School, Kenilworth Rd, Leamington Spa
51 Sibford School, Sibford Ferris, Banbury
52 Park School, Queens Park South Drive, Bournemouth
53 Nook Lane Junior School, Nook Lane, Stannington, Sheffield
54 Cowbridge Comprehensive School, Aberthin Rd, Cowbridge
55 Llandrindod Wells CP School, Powys
56 Support for Learning, Early Intervention Service. London Borough of Hounslow
57 Hounslow Heath Infant and Nursery School, Martindale Rd, Hounslow
58 Sparrow Farm Junior School, Sparrow Farm Drive, Feltham
59 Green Dragon Primary School, North Rd, Brentford
60 Cavendish Primary School, Edensor Rd, London
61 William Hogarth Primary School, Duke Rd, Chiswick, London
62 St Mary's School, Bateman St, Cambridge
63 Dame Bradbury's School, Ashdon Rd, Saffron Walden
64 Salesian Sixth Form College, Chertsey, Surrey
65 Bedstone College, Bucknell, Shropshire
66 City of Bath College

I am extremely grateful to all the people who helped in the collection of data for the tests and all the pupils, students and adults who took the tests. A huge 'Thank you'.

References

Ackerman, P.T. and Dykman, R.A. (1996) 'Reading-disabled students with and without comorbid arithmetic disability', *Developmental Neuropsychology*, 11, 351–371.

Alloway, T.P. (2011) *Improving Working Memory*, London: Sage.

Ashcraft, M., Kirk, E.P. and Hopko, D. (1998) On the cognitive consequences of mathematics anxiety. In Donlan, C. (ed.) *The Development of Mathematical Skills*, Hove: The Psychological Corporation.

Ashlock, R.B. (2009) *Error Patterns in Computation. Using Error Patterns to Help Each Student Learn*, Boston, MA: Allyn and Bacon.

Ashlock, R.B., Johnson, M.L., Wilson, et al. (1983) *Guiding Each Child's Learning of Mathematics.* Columbus, OH: Merrill.

Austin, J.D. (1982) Children with learning difficulties in mathematics, *School Science and Mathematics*, 82(3), 201–208.

Bath, J.B., Chinn, S.J. and Knox, D.E. (1986) *The Test of Cognitive Style in Mathematics*, East Aurora, NY: Slosson.

Boaler, J. (2009) *The Elephant in the Classroom*, London: Souvenir Press.

Bransford, J.D., Brown, A.L. and Cocking, R.R. (eds) (2000) *How People Learn*, Washington, DC: National Academy Press.

Brueckner, C.K., and Bond, G.L. (1955) *The Diagnosis and Treatment of Learning Difficulties*, New York: Appleton-Century-Crofts.

Bryant, D.P., Bryant, B.R. and Hammill, D.D. (2000) 'Characteristic behaviours of students with LD who have teacher-identified math weaknesses', *Journal of Learning Disabilities*, 33, no. 2, 168–177. 199.

Buswell, G.T. and Judd, C.M. (1925) Summary of educational investigations relating to arithmetic. *Supplementary Educational Monographs*, Chicago: University of Chicago Press.

Butterworth, B. (1999) *The Mathematical Brain*, London: Macmillan.

Butterworth, B. (2003) *The Dyscalculia Screener*, London: GL Assessment.

Confederation of British Industry (CBI) (2006) Lacking in skills, *The Times*, 26 June.

Chinn, S.J. (1991) Factors to consider when designing a test protocol in mathematics for dyslexics. In Snowling, M. and Thomson, M. (eds) *Dyslexia: Integrating Theory and Practice,* London: Whurr, 253–258.

Chinn, S.J. (1994) 'A study of the basic number fact skills of children from specialist dyslexic and 'mainstream' schools', *Dyslexia Review*, 2, 4–6.

Chinn, S.J. (1995) 'A pilot study to compare aspects of arithmetic skill', *Dyslexia Review*, 4, 4–7.

Chinn, S.J. (1996) 'The relationship between the grades achieved in GCSE mathematics by 26 male students and their scores on the WISC', *Dyslexia Review*, 7, 8–9.

Chinn, S. (2008) 'Mathematics anxiety in secondary students in England', *Dyslexia*, 15, 61–68.

Chinn, S. (2009) 'Mathematics anxiety in secondary students in England', *Dyslexia*, 15, 61–68.

Chinn, S. (2010) 'The illusion of learning', *Dyslexia Review*, 21, 7–10.

Chinn, S. (2012) *The Trouble with Maths*, 2nd edn. Abingdon: Routledge.

Chinn, S.J. and Ashcroft, J.R. (1993) *Mathematics for Dyslexics: A Teaching Handbook*, London, Whurr.

Chinn, S.J. and Ashcroft, J.R. (2007) *Mathematics for Dyslexics: Including Dyscalculia*, 3rd edn. London: Whurr.

Coben, D. (2003) *Adult Numeracy: Review of Research and Related Literature*, London: NRDC.

Cohen, M. (1997) *The Children's Memory Scale*, London: Psychological Corporation.

Datta, D.K. and Scarfpin, J.A. (1983) 'Types of math anxiety', *Math Notebook*, (CLTM) 3, 9–10.

Devlin, K. (2000) *The Maths Gene*, London: Weidenfeld and Nicholson.

DfEE (1999) *The National Numeracy Strategy: Framework for Teaching Mathematics: Reception to Year 6*, London: DfEE.

DfES (2001) *The National Numeracy Strategy. Guidance to Support Learners with Dyslexia and Dyscalculia*, London: DFES.

Engelhardt, J.M. (1977) 'Analysis of children's computational errors: a quantitative approach', *British Journal of Educational Psychology*, 47, 149–154.

France, N. (1979) *The Profile of Mathematical Skills*, Windsor: NFER-Nelson. [Out of print.]

Gathercole, S. and Alloway, T.P. (2008) *Working Memory and Learning*, London: SAGE.

Gathercole, S.E., Alloway, T.P. and Kirkwood, H.J. (2008) *The Working Memory Rating Scale*, London: Psychological Corporation.

Geary, D. (2004) 'Mathematics and learning disabilities', *Journal of Learning Disabilities*, 37, 4–15.

Geary, D.C. (2010) Missouri longitudinal study of mathematical development and disability. In Cowan, R., Saxton, M. and Tolmie A, (eds) *Understanding Number Development and Number Difficulties (No. 7, British Journal of Educational Psychology, Monograph Series II: Psychological Aspects of Education - Current Trends)*, Leicester: British Psychological Society, 31–49.

Gersten, R., Jordan N.C. and Flojo, J.R. (2005) Early identification and interventions for students with mathematics difficulties, *Journal of Learning Disabilities*, 38(4), 293–304.

Girling, M. (2001) 'Towards a definition of basic numeracy', *Mathematics Teaching*, 174, 12–13.

Gray, E. and Tall, D. (1994) 'Duality, ambiguity and flexibility: a 'proceptual' view of simple arithmetic', *Journal of Research into Mathematics Education*, 25, no. 2, 116–140.

Hadfield, O.D. and McNeil, K. (1994) 'The relationship between Myers-Briggs personality type and mathematics anxiety among pre-service elementary teachers', *Journal of Instructional Psychology*, 21, no. 4, 375–384.

Hattie, J.A.C. (2009) *Visible Learning*, London: Routledge.

Hodgen, J., Brown, M., Kuchemann, D. et al. (2010) Mathematical attainment of English secondary school students: a 30-year comparison. *BERA Symposium*.

Hofmeister, A. (1975) Integrating criterion-referenced testing into instruction. In Hively, W. and Reynolds, M. (eds) *Domain-referenced Testing in Special Education*, Reston, VA: Council on Exceptional Children, 77–88.

Houtkoop, W. and Jones, S. (1999). Adult numeracy: an international comparison. In Van Groenestijn, M. and Coben D. (eds) *Mathematics as Part of Lifelong Learning: Proceedings of the Fifth International Conference of Adults Learning Maths – A Research Forum, ALM-5*, London: Goldsmiths College, University of London in association with ALM, 32–40.

Johnston-Wilder, S. (2008) 'What makes a good mathematics teacher?' *Education Guardian*, 30 September.

Kavale, K.A. and Forness, S.R. (2000) 'What definitions of learning disabilities say and don't say', *Journal of Learning Disabilities*, 33, 239–256.

Keeler, M.L. and Swanson, H.L. (2001) 'Does strategy knowledge influence working memory in children with mathematical difficulties?', *Journal of Learning Disabilities*, 43, no. 5, 418–434.

Kho Tek, H., Yen Shu, M. and Lim, J. (2009) *The Singapore Model Method for Learning Mathematics*, Singapore, Ministry of Education.

Koppitz, M.E. (1997) *Visual Aural Digit Span Test (VADS)*, London: Pearson.

Kubiszyn, T. and Borich, G. (2007) *Educational Testing and Measurement*, 8th edn, Hoboken, NJ: John Wiley.

Lane, C. and Chinn, S.J. (1986) 'Learning by self-voice echo', *Academic Therapy*, 21, 477–481.

Lowe, P.A. and Lee, S.W. (2005) *The Test Anxiety Inventory for Children and Adolescents*, Kansas: University of Kansas.

Lundberg, I. and Sterner, G. (2006) 'Reading, arithmetic and task orientation – how are they related?', *Annal of Dyslexia*, 56, 361–377.

Mabbott, D.J. and Bisanz, J. (2008) 'Computational skills, working memory and conceptual knowledge in older children with mathematics learning disabilities', *Journal of Learning Disabilities*, 41, 15–28.

Nunes, T., Bryant, P. and Watson, A. (2009) *Key Understandings in Mathematics Learning*, London: Nuffield Foundation.

Ofsted (2006) *Evaluation of Maths Provision for 14-19 year-olds*, HM2611 (HYPERLINK "http://www.ofsted.gov.uk" www.ofsted.gov.uk).

Ostad, S.A. (1997) 'Developmental difficulties in addition strategies. A comparison of mathematically disabled and mathematically normal children', *British Journal of Educational Psychology*, 67, 345–357.

Parmar, R.S. and Cawley, J.F. (1997) 'Preparing teachers to teach mathematics to students with learning disabilities', *Journal of Learning Disabilities*, 30, 188–197.

Primary School Curriculum, Ireland (1999) Dublin, Government Publications.

Ramaa, S. and Gowramma, J.P. (2002) 'A systematic procedure for identifying and classifying children with dyscalculia among primary school children in India, *Dyslexia*, 8, 67–85.

Rashid, S. and Brooks, G. (2010) *The Levels of Attainment in Literacy and Numeracy for 13–19 Year-Olds in England, 1948–2009*, London: NRDC.

Richardson, F.C. and Shuinn, R.M. (1972) 'The mathematics anxiety rating scale', *Journal of Counselling Psychology*, 19, 551–554.

Riding, R.J. and Rayner, S. (1998) *Cognitive Style and Learning Strategies*, London: David Fulton.

Russell, R.L. and Ginsburg, H.P. (1984) 'Cognitive analysis of children's mathematics difficulties', *Cognition and Instruction*, 1, 217–244.

Salvia, J. and Ysseldyke, J.E. (1988) *Assessment in Special and Remedial Education*, 4th edn, Boston, MA: Houghton Mifflin.

Seligman, M.E.P. (1998) *Learned Optimism*, New York: Pocket Books.

Sharma, M.C. (1985) Mathematics as a second language, *Math Notebook*, CTLM.

Skemp, R.R. (1971) *The Psychology of Learning Mathematics*, Harmondsworth: Penguin.

Skemp, R.R. (1986) *The Psychology of Learning Mathematics*, 2nd edn, Harmondsworth: Penguin.

Thambirajah, M.S. (2011) *Developmental Assessment of the School-aged Child with Developmental Disabilities*, London: Jessica Kingsley.

The National Numeracy Strategy. Framework for teaching mathematics from Reception to Year 6. (1999) Department for Education and Employment.

Tilton, J.W. (1947) 'Individualized and meaningful instruction in arithmetic', *Journal of Educational Psychology*, 38, no. 2, 83–88.

Trujillo, K.M. and Hadfield, O.D. (1999) 'Tracing the roots of mathematical anxiety through in-depth interviews with pre-service elementary teachers', *College Students' Journal*, 33(2), 219–233.

Underhill, R.G., Uprichard, A.E. and Heddens, J.W. (1980) *Diagnosing Mathematical Difficulties*, Columbus, OH: Charles E Merrill.

US Department of Education (2008) *Foundations for Success: The Final Report of the National Mathematics Advisory Panel*. www2.ed.gov/about/bdscomm/list/mathpanel/report/final-report.pdf

Westwood P. (2000) *Numeracy and Learning Difficulties*, London: Fulton.

Whitaker Sena, J.D., Lowe, P.A. and Lee, S.W. (2007) 'Significant predictors of test anxiety among students with and without learning disabilities', *Journal of Learning Disabilities*, 40, 360–376.

Zaslavsky C. (1999) *Fear of Math*, New Brunswick, NJ: Rutgers University Press.

Index

www.routledge.com/education

The Trouble with Maths
A Practical Guide to Helping Learners with Numeracy Difficulties, 2nd Edition

Steve Chinn, Education Consultant, UK

Now in a second edition, the award-winning *The Trouble with Maths* offers important insights into the often confusing world of numeracy. By looking at learning difficulties in maths from several perspectives, including the language of mathematics, thinking styles and the demands of individual topics, this book offers a complete overview of the most common problems associated with mathematics teaching and learning. It draws on tried-and-tested methods based on research and the author's many years of classroom experience to provide an authoritative yet highly accessible one-stop classroom resource.

Combining advice, guidance and practical activities, this user-friendly guide will enable you to:

- develop flexible thinking skills;
- use alternative strategies for pupils to access basic facts;
- understand the implications of pre-requisite skills, such as working memory, on learning;
- implement effective preventative measures before disaffection sets in;
- recognise maths anxiety and tackle self-esteem problems;
- tackle the difficulties with word problems that many pupils may have;
- select appropriate materials to enhance understanding.

With useful features such as checklists for the evaluation of books, an outline for setting up an inclusive Maths Department policy and a brand new chapter on materials, manipulatives and communication, this book will equip you with the essential skills to tackle your pupils' maths difficulties and improve standards. This book will be useful for all teachers, classroom assistants, learning support assistants and parents who have pupils who underachieve with maths.

PB: 978-0-415-67010-4

For more information and to order a copy visit
www.routledge.com/9780415670104

Available from all good bookshops